THE POEMS OF

CATULLUS

· THE POEMS OF ·

CATULLUS

Translated by

CHARLES MARTIN

THE JOHNS HOPKINS UNIVERSITY PRESS

BALTIMORE AND LONDON

This book has been brought to publication
with the generous assistance of
the David M. Robinson Publication Fund.

Johns Hopkins Paperbacks edition, 1990
4 6 8 9 7 5 3

A limited edition of these poems was published
by Abattoir Editions, The University of
Nebraska at Omaha, in 1979.

The Johns Hopkins University Press
2715 North Charles Street
Baltimore, Maryland 21218-4363
The Johns Hopkins Press Ltd., London

LIBRARY OF CONGRESS
CATALOGING-IN-PUBLICATION DATA
Catullus, Gaius Valerius.
  [Works. English. 1990]
  The poems of Catullus / translated by Charles
Martin.
    p. cm.
  "A limited edition of these poems was published
by Abattoir Editions, the University of Nebraska at
Omaha, in 1979"—T.p. verso.
  ISBN 0-8018-3925-4. — ISBN 0-8018-3926-2 (pbk.)
  1. Catullus, Gaius Valerius—Translations,
English. I. Martin, Charles, 1942– . II. Title.
PA6275.E5M28 1990
874'.01—dc20   89-45486
                                            CIP

A catalog record for this book is available from the
British Library.

To
Robert Hass
and
Charles Molesworth

· CONTENTS ·

1

Near the end of the seventeenth century, John Dryden could speak of translation, with offhanded assurance, as the act of bringing the thought of one author over into the language of another. In his day, poetic thought was social in nature, as were the rhymed couplets in which it was expressed. As a result, the poet was linked in thought and expression not only to the community of the living but to the *fabulae Manes* as well, the fabled dead of the literary tradition, whose collective wisdom he guarded and interpreted.

Today, nearly three hundred years after Dryden, we speak of a poet's voice rather than a poet's thought, and we require that voice to be a reflection of the poet's sensibility rather than an expression of the tradition from which it emerges: our poet must deliver original, subjective truths in idiosyncratic utterances. We no longer share Dryden's sense of the wholeness of the past or of its continuity with the present: the modern poet has more in common with the archeologist in the ruins than with the curator of the museum. And, not surprisingly, we give our almost automatic assent to Robert Frost's intimidating proposition that poetry is what gets lost in the translation. As how could it not, when any voice, poetic or otherwise, shares in the evanescence of gesture?

It is the voice part of poetry that is so easily lost in translation.

2

Catullus entered Latin poetry as a voice not at all like those that the ears of his fellow citizens were used to hearing. In Rome during the first century B.C., a long-established tradition of high-minded, so-cially responsible, didactic verse was being challenged by a new wave from the East. Inspired by the classical postmodernism of Alexandrian poetry, a group of poets known today as the neoterics were writing poems that were playfully cerebral, sophisticated in their sensuality, and emphatically subjective. Nothing like this had happened to Latin verse before this happened to it; and so, when his first audience discovered Catullus among the neoterics, he must have been as much of a shock to his fellow citizens as the early twentieth-century modernists were to ours.

There really had been no one like Catullus writing in Latin before he came along, though he was not original in our sense of the word, which usually implies that a poet so labelled has neither read nor acknowledged the work of either his predecessors or his contemporaries. Catullus was typically neoteric in his erudition, and his voice was certainly shaped by his predecessors, the Latin and Greek poets whose works he carefully studied; nevertheless, what they had done was very different from what he would do.

One important difference, and one of the major reasons he is so attractive a poet in our time, is his way of presenting himself as one voice among other voices—highly competitive, yes, but not privileged, not central to his culture, as the epic poet believes himself to be. Whatever attention his poems get is attention that they have to put up a fight for, which is perhaps why these poems seem so active, with all their questions and answers, projections and provocations. Their author is one poet for whom solitude seems to have had little if any charm. We usually think of writing as a solitary act, but even here Catullus surprises us—in poem 50, we find him composing verses in the company of his friend, Calvus. When he is alone in these poems, his ordinary response is to issue an invitation of one kind or another. One kind invites someone to visit the poet:

> Go, poem, pay a call on Caecilius,
> my friend the master of erotic verses:
> tell him to leave his lakefront place at Comum
> & spend a little time here at Verona. . . .

Another kind requests an invitation from someone else:

> I beg of you, my sweet, my Ipsitilla,
> my darling, my sophisticated beauty,
> summon me to a midday assignation. . . .

Although he said things that no one else would ever say, in ways that no one else could say them, he was also fascinated by the kind of things that other people were always saying, by the extraordinary range of the social registers of the collective Roman voice. Proverbs and clichés, the featureless coins of everyday speech, easily made their way into his verse: Does Dickface fornicate? *The pot gathers its own potherbs.* Aemilius thinks himself clever? *He hasn't the brains to guide a miller's donkey.* (In an age when there were millers, and the millers had donkeys, the latter would move endlessly in a circle around the millstone that ground grain into flour; who could not figure out the route would have been dumb indeed.) Does some poor *nouveau* attempt to put on airs by trying to mouth words as he has heard the nobs pronounce them? Catullus is on hand in poem 84 to deflate such pretensions:

> Arrius had to have aitches to swell his orations,
>   and threatened us all with, *"hawful, hinsidious hach-shuns!"*

In poem 53, he captures the spontaneously indecent observation of an anonymous bystander, overheard at one of the city's open-air courts while the poet's diminutive friend Calvus was orating: "Great gods, this little pecker's sure persuasive!"

Much of the time he wrote a poetry whose strength and attractiveness derives from its openness to the life and language of the streets of Rome and Verona. To paraphrase Paolo Pasolini on Ezra Pound, Catullus' love for the purely phatic aspect of language, its function as chat, is one of the most extraordinary phenomena in classical literature. Gossip enthralls him: he is the poet as representative ear, the not-so-still center of a maelstrom of voices; why, this one will listen to stories about anyone from any source—even, as in poem 67, from a door anxious to disburden itself of a few unsavory secrets. And, of course, he will pass the stuff along to others; why on earth would he keep it to himself? A good story repaid an invitation to dinner, deflated a rival, made you appear more serious, more attractive, or more dangerous in company. Catullus is skilled at passing gossip on with a kind of disclaimer: "Gellius, what shall I tell them? Everyone's asking me why it is that you . . ." He presents himself as someone who knows just what everyone's saying:

> What everyone says of pretentious, babbling asses
> fits you, if anyone, putrescent Victius. . . .

He is wonderfully good at lining up imaginary tropes for real battles, battles in which there is no muck too messy to fling at an enemy, including the sort of messages scratched into walls about people like "RUFA THE BOLOGNESE WIFE OF MENENIUS," whose unsavory activities in the cemetery live on long after her in poem 59.

Behind the grotesque, boastful exaggerations of the obscenities, there is often—though not always—a more serious purpose, for Catullus sees himself as a moralist, an arbiter of conviviality, who must often remind others of what constitutes proper behavior in social relationships. In order to make any impression at all on the morally dense, those reminders often had to be pretty savage. Nevertheless, the street fighter rolling up his cloak into a shield does so in order to protect a curious, almost childlike innocent, who is easily (and repeatedly) disappointed because of the high expectations he has for the behavior of others. Catullus believes absolutely in some kind of moral authority apart from and above mere self-interest. That authority resides in such deities as *Fides,* the Roman god of Good Faith, *Nemesis,* the Greek god of retribution, and, ultimately, in the nameless abstractions he calls upon in poem 76, when he wishes to be delivered from the self-described sickness of his passion for Lesbia.

There, as in other poems, with unself-conscious ease Catullus could turn from the pungent obscenities of the streets, from language used in exaggeration, to the ritual pieties of religious expression, in search of another kind of language for his poems, a language whose balance and restraint will redress grievances and help to set the moral universe in order.

3

Of course, if he had been content to say only what everyone else was saying, it is very unlikely that we would be reading him today: his almost miraculous survival was surely the work of an editor who recognized and valued the uniqueness of his gift, passing it on to a long succession of readers who have had the same high regard for it. The uniqueness of any poet whom we find interesting as a person lies in the success with which he or she manages to imprint a communal poetics with the stamp of subjectivity, with what we have been calling the poet's voice.

Catullus is so often immediately accessible to the reader that we tend to think of him as simple, direct, and unaffected; these are, after all, words that are frequently used as terms of praise for a poet nowadays. Most of the time, however, they simply do not apply to Catullus, whose voice and sensibility are more accurately described as complex, duplicitous, artful, and ironic. He is almost always saying more than just one thing. Consider, for example, poem 3, his lament for the dead sparrow of his mistress, which begins with what seems a solemn invocation:

> *Lugete, o Veneres Cupidinesque*
> *et quantum est hominum venustiorum!*

> Cry out lamenting, Venuses & Cupids,
> and mortal men endowed with Love's refinement!

But how solemn can this invocation be when the very next line, *"Passer mortuus est meae puellae . . . ,"* reveals the somewhat less than portentous reason behind it: "The sparrow of my ladyfriend is dead." Venuses and Cupids (the plural is meant to suggest the enormity of the poet's grief) are urgently summoned (along with the more refined among mortals) to grieve over the hardly unprecedented death of yet another avatar of the common sparrow, *Passer domesticus*. Does he really mean it? The short answer—there being insufficient room in this introduction for the long answer—is Yes and no, or He does and he doesn't: the playfulness of this poem, as of so many others, makes a direct, unequivocal answer impossible to give.

The main strategy of playfulness is ironic juxtaposition, as in the juxtaposition of high summons and low motive in the opening lines. But here, as elsewhere in the verse of Catullus, there are ironic juxtapositions even on the level of diction. There is, for instance, the line in which he describes the sparrow lighting out for the underworld: *"qui nunc it per iter tenebricosum."* Just eleven syllables: in the first six, we can hear the sparrow chirping along in the poet's own words, an understandably nervous, repetitive, obsessively rhyming little scrap of sensibility: *"qui nunc it per iter."* Suddenly, out of nowhere comes the second half of the line, a single, polysyllabic monstrosity that stops the bird dead in its tracks: "TENE-BRICOSUM!" "It now flits off on its way, goes GLOOM-LADEN . . ." tries, not without losing something, to catch the effect.

Other gestures of his voice are even less possible to reproduce in English. What can a translator do about the opening line of poem 12, against Marrucinus Asinius? At dinner parties, his left hand goes slipping over into his neighbor's lap: Is he just being friendly? No—a moment later, and neighbor's napkin is missing. Catullus pins him to the board with a line that forever marries his name to his left-handed proclivities:

Marrucin' Asini, manu sinistra . . .

There is the pattern made by the repetition of the three vowel sounds (*a u i / a i i / a u i / i a*), and there is the repetition of all but two of the consonants; there is the insinuating rhyme of name and hand, *Marru'* and *manu*, not to mention the wicked repetition, like gossip being passed on in a whisper from one ear to another, of *cin'*

/ *Asini* / *sini;* and there is the way in which they together build, in only as much time as it takes to mouth those four words, an unanswerable equation: Asinius is sinister.

4

Catullus is a poet with a wide range of experience: he not only knows life on the streets but has mastered his craft, is a well-taught student of literature and mythology, and an intimate of the rich, the powerful, and the famous. In his poetry he is unwilling to scant any aspect of that experience in favor of any other. He is capable of juxtaposing an ancient cliché with a figure drawn from the world of Roman high finance or from Alexandrian literature. Consider, for example, poem 7, a lyric for Lesbia that begins:

> *Quaeris quot mihi basiationes*
> *tuae, Lesbia, sint satis superque.*

> My Lesbia, you ask how many kisses
> would be enough to satisfy, to sate me!

Lesbia has asked Catullus a straightforward question to which this poem is going to be the answer. Or is it? It may indeed be an answer, but it is anything but straightforward. The signal is given with that word *basiationes*, for which the English "kisses" is a woefully pale shadow. Something's already lost in translation, and the poem will lose a little more, since the whole phrase, broken between two lines, *basiationes* / *tuae*, probably sounded as odd in Latin as the corresponding English phrase, "basiations of you," would sound to us. Yes, there is such a word as "basiation," lovingly laid up in the Oxford English Dictionary, after having been used, once, by George Meredith in 1879. However, the word is perfectly useless to any sane translator, since it's obvious that Meredith got it from Catullus in the first place; translation ought to be a matter of repaying a debt rather than increasing it, and so, alas, kisses must do.

If the poem has already, in its first two lines, taken something of a leap away from the straightforward, it gets even more indirect when it answers, or appears to answer, Lesbia's question. The first part of the poet's answer is given in a poetic cliché as old as Homer or the Bible, and probably not exactly a novelty then, either:

quam magnus numerus Libyssae harenae,

as many kisses as there are grains of sand in the Libyan desert. But immediately Catullus goes on to complicate things:

. . . Laserpiciferis iacet Cyrenis,
oraclum Iovis inter aestuosi
et Batti veteris sacrum sepulcrum. . . .

. . . near Cyrene, where silphium is gathered,
between the shrine of Jupiter the sultry
& the venerable sepulchre of Battus!

The playful self-mockery that offers us *basiationes / tuae*, makes Catullus also capable of ironically posing to his mistress as the modern successor of the overeducated Alexandrians. Here is one who not only knows the site of the commercial center for the trade in asafoetida but gives the coordinates of that site with a detail that translates into a literary reference: Callimachus, the pluperfect Alexandrian, to whom Catullus was especially devoted, came from Cyrene and called himself Battiades, son of Battus, the founder of the city. Not only does the poet know all of these things, but he is perfectly capable of including such details in what is sometimes taken as a simple love poem. A love poem it is, but simple it is not; and much of its complexity comes from the poet's need to join together, for the moment at least—and not without the serious qualification of irony—the disparate parts of his own experience.

5

Neither his concern nor his strategies will be unfamiliar to those who have read the English poets of the seventeenth century, especially John Donne, with whom Catullus shares the ability to conceive of a conceit whose intellectual brilliance reflects the intensity of his emotions. He does this never more perfectly than in poem 5:

> Vivamus, mea Lesbia, atque amemus,
> rumoresque senum severiorum
> omnes unius aestimemus assis.
> Soles occidere et redire possunt:
> nobis, cum semel occidit brevis lux,
> nox est perpetua una dormienda.
> Da mi basia mille, deinde centum,
> dein mille altera, dein secunda centum,
> deinde usque altera mille, deinde centum,
> dein, cum milia multa fecerimus,
> conturbabimus illa, ne sciamus,
> aut ne quis malus invidire possit,
> cum tantum sciat esse basiorum.
>
> Lesbia, let us live only for loving,
> and let us value at a single penny
> all the loose flap of senile busybodies!
> Suns when they set are capable of rising,
> but at the setting of our own brief light
> night is one sleep from which we never waken.
> Give me a thousand kisses, then a hundred,
> another thousand next, another hundred,
> a thousand without pause & then a hundred,
> until when we have run up our thousands
> we will cry bankrupt, hiding our assets
> from ourselves & any who would harm us,
> knowing the volume of our trade in kisses.

The poem is an invitation from the poet to his beloved to escape with him from the traditional restraints imposed upon them by Roman society (represented by the gossipmongering elders) and to live entirely for the moment, entirely for the sake of passion. (Is it a shared passion? The reader may very well wonder, for Catullus is anything but explicit here.)

Nevertheless the premise of the poem is that such an escape is indeed possible, and Catullus is wonderfully persuasive here: his voice caresses the Latin, plays with it as who had ever had the wit to do before him? When he wants to illustrate the brevity of life and the longlastingness of death, he takes advantage of the similarity in sound of the Latin words for light and night, *lux* and *nox*. (Here, perhaps, is one of the rare cases where a little something is actually gained in translation, since the rhyme in English is more exact than in Latin.) The *lux* goes out at the end of the fifth line, and *nox* begins at the very beginning of the sixth, which sets that monosyllable in poignant opposition to the polysyllabic words that tell us what it really represents:

> *nox est perpetua una dormienda.*

Catullus here takes brilliant advantage of the elision that occurs in Latin verse when an unstressed vowel ends a word coming before a word that begins with a vowel, as between *perpetua* and *una;* the last vowel of the first word is omitted, and so the line would actually have been pronounced as:

> *nox est perpetu' una dormienda,*

joining *perpetua,* "forever," and *una,* "one," into a single cry, a lament for the unending sleep of death.

Nevertheless, against this blissful vision of erotic liberation from the moral restraints imposed by society, the poet sets a very distinctive countermovement, beginning in the third line, where he does not tell us that the rumors generated by the old men are worthless but rather tells us (with a curiously odd precision) that they are not worth an *as,* the Roman equivalent of our penny. This is not remarkable in itself, but then, when he asks Lesbia for kisses, he does so by alternating demands for a thousand kisses (*mille*) with demands for a hundred (*centum*) in a way that would have inevitably reminded his audience of fingers shuttling across the columns of an abacus, busily toting up sums in some Roman counting house:

da mi basia mille   deinde centum,
dein mille altera   dein secunda centum,
deinde usque altera mille   deinde centum,

What is he up to here? In his edition of Catullus, Kenneth Quinn suggests that "*da mi* + name of article + quantity was perhaps the formula for placing an order with a merchant (hence *basia mille*, not *mille basia*). We are invited perhaps to imagine the kisses stacked in rows (like sacks of grain, say) as the quantities specified are delivered—and then jumbled up into a single pile." (Quinn, p. 109) Kisses delivered like sacks of grain, then, with someone keeping track of the deliveries on an abacus. If Quinn's suggestion seems bizarre, it is only because we have simplified Catullus for too long. John Donne, addressing his mistress as "[M]y America, my new found land," would have had no problem with the conceit. Quinn is—no pun intended—right on the money here, for when Catullus finishes his sums, he proposes to throw them into confusion, so that no one will ever know the total. But the word he uses, *conturbare*, is, according to C. J. Fordyce, "a technical term for fraudulent bankruptcy with concealment of assets." (Fordyce, p. 107) Such language in a love poem must have seemed as curious to his audience as, say, a poem in which a love affair is compared to a leveraged buy-out would be to us.

Nevertheless, the language is indisputably there. Catullus did not allow this theme to enter the poem by accident, and its effect on the poem is to contradict the ostensible message of the poet to his mistress: a poem which at first seems to defy calculation, to throw calculation to the winds, is in fact inextricably bound to the very instrument of calculation, the abacus. And, finally, what are we to make of that word *conturbare?* Does it not convey the disturbing intimation that somewhere down the road, emotional ruin, a bankruptcy of the spirit, is lying in wait for the optimistic lover?

6

Immensely popular for a few centuries after his death, Catullus' work disappeared almost completely in the early Middle Ages; it survived only because of the discovery of a manuscript of his poems at Verona about the year 1300. (Were it not for that manuscript, we would have only poem 62, which was preserved independently.) Poetic influence is very often indirect: Dante Alighieri does not mention Catullus or his poems, though in Sirmione there is a castle, once the property of Dante's great friend Can Grande della Scala, which Dante is said to have visited. Had he walked a mile or so to the end of the peninsula, he could have sat in the ruins of the villa known today as *le grotte di Catullo*. There he might have recited to himself parts of the *Commedia*, which, like many of the poems Catullus wrote, is written in lines of eleven syllables: Dante inherited and shaped a line which Catullus before him had inherited from the poets of Alexandria; after demonstrating its usefulness, Catullus passed it on to other Latin poets, whose work and influence survived into Dante's time. The Italian poets of Dante's age were of great interest to the poets of the English Renaissance, and so the line of eleven syllables (shortened to ten) became one of the continental sources of the ever dependable, ever renewable workhorse of English poetry, the iambic pentameter line: Catullus enters English poetry already lost in translation.

In a more explicit way, Catullus appears on the English scene at the beginning of its Renaissance, in an enormous, sprawly, mock-serious elegy inspired by his two sparrow poems: John Skelton's *The Boke of Phyllyp Sparrowe*. After Skelton, virtually every important poet of the sixteenth and seventeenth centuries who read Latin knew Catullus, but his influence was subterranean enough to make him something of "a poet's poet."

One reason for this was that Callus had gotten off to such a late start. The manuscript that surfaced in Verona was found before Gutenberg's useful invention, and so it took considerable time before its poems could be copied and gotten into circulation in Europe, and of course, even longer for them to find their way to England. Moreover, those poems appeared without the centuries of interpretive commentary that had led to the canonization of poets like Virgil and Horace. In the meanwhile, the neoteric tradition had been lost, and its assumptions were no longer intelligible. As a result, some of the poems, such as poem 64, were very difficult to deal with. Since there were no other poems like this one, the question, What kind of a poem is this? was impossible to answer.

The poet's reception was also slowed down by English prudishness in the face of Catullan licentiousness. In the eyes of the guardians of public morality from the 1600s through the 1800s, the morals of classical authors (with the exceptions of Virgil and Horace) were frequently thought to be unfit to set before children. But our poet was really the worst offender: as Byron's Donna Inez hendecasyllabically opined, "Catullus scarcely has a decent poem." This did not mean that he could not be read, only that hypocrisy made pleasure pay for the privilege, as Byron shows us in his description of the classical education of the young Don Juan:

> Juan was taught from out the best edition,
>   Expurgated by learned men, who place,
> Judiciously, from out the schoolboy's vision,
>   The grosser part; but, fearful to deface
> Too much their modest bard by this omission,
>   And, pitying sore his mutilated case,
> They only add them in an appendix,
> Which saves, in fact, the trouble of an index;
>
> For there we have them all "at one fell swoop,"
>   Instead of being scattered through the pages;
> They stand forth, marshalled in a handsome troop,
>   To meet the ingenuous youth of future ages. . . .

The ingenuous youth of our age might well be disappointed: one recent edition of the poems of Catullus intended for the edification of young scholars not only left out a fourth of the poems, but omitted an appendix as well.

7

Catullus is perhaps the only Latin poet of the classical period to have had an important influence on modern poetry in English, and it is not unreasonable to regard Ezra Pound as the modern discoverer of Catullus, at least for poets writing in English, since he did so much to encourage the young modernists to read and translate the Latin poet.

As George Steiner has pointed out, however, Pound's judgement had been formed by the poets and translators of the nineteenth century. It was, in fact, J. W. Mackail, eminent man of letters (O.M., M.A., LL.D., F.B.A.), in his standard text, *Latin Literature* (1895), who first saw in Catullus what the moderns were later to see, praising his "hard clear verse" and the "clear and almost terrible simplicity that puts Catullus in a place by himself among the Latin poets. Where others labour in the ore of thought and gradually forge it out into sustained expression, he sees with a single glance, and does not strike a second time." (Mackail, pp. 57, 61) A high regard for simplicity is certainly not the virtue I would choose to stress for readers of Catullus, but Mackail's appreciation does have a hard, clear, modern ring to it.

And Ezra Pound, himself searching for hardness and clarity in verse, found it in Catullus, whom he read with close attention during the years when he was one of the inventers of free verse. Pound was fascinated by the way in which Catullus had transformed the matter and meter of Sappho in his poem 51; and, setting out from some rather wooden imitations of that poem, he very quickly learned how to write a poem in Sapphics that sounded as though it were *vers libre:*

> Golden rose the house, in the portal I saw
> thee, a marvel, carven in subtle stuff, a
> portent. Life died down in the lamp and flickered,
> caught at the wonder.

The traditional Sapphic line breaks after the fifth or sixth syllable, and is, to a large extent, end-stopped. "Apparuit" sounds like free verse because Pound has enjambed the lines and paused within them at unpredictable places. What I have said about the first stanza of this poem is true of the rest of it. After mastering the Sapphic stanza, Pound fragmented it to create "The Return," a poem in which Sapphics really do meet free verse:

> See, they return; ah, see the tentative
> Movements, and the slow feet,
> The trouble in the pace and the uncertain
> Wavering!

Little of the Catullan influence manages to make its way into Pound's later work, but it is clear that the influence was extraordinarily important to him in his formative years. Pound seems to be paying homage to it in Canto III, where he lovingly evokes the beauty of Sirmione in the passage beginning "Gods float in the azure air," and which concludes with two lines that are a commentary on the first tableau of poem 64:

> And in the water, the almond-white swimmers,
> The silvery water glazes the upturned nipple. . . .

Catullus was an influence not only on the formation of free verse in our time, but on the development of traditional verse as well. Robert Frost was a lifelong admirer of Catullus, and you can hear the influence of Catullan hendecasyllabics on Frost's iambic pentameter, which often admits an eleventh syllable to the line. Frost wrote a poem, "For Once, Then, Something," in which he imitated Catullan hendecasyllablic meter in a way that gives us, for once, then, a clear sound of the measure part of the poet's voice:

> Others taunt me with having knelt at well-curbs
> Always wrong to the light, so never seeing
> Deeper down in the well than where the water
> Gives me back in a shining surface picture
> Me myself in the summer heaven, godlike,
> Looking out of a wreath of fern and cloud puffs.

It is not at all accidental, I think, that the two poets who have made the greatest use of Catullus in our time and our language saw in him a source of renewal.

8

In our time, poetic translation into English has been distinguished by the variety of its achievements, ranging from the strict, prosaic, almost word-for-word accuracies of Vladimir Nabokov's version of *Eugene Onegin* to Robert Lowell's *Imitations* and Christopher Logue's *War Music*, both of which achieve brilliant results by taking the greatest imaginable liberties with their originals.

Nevertheless, the terms of translation have really not changed since the time of John Dryden, who first named and described Nabokov's approach to his text as metaphrase, or word-for-word translation. In his *Preface to Ovid's Epistles Translated*, he also described what Lowell and Logue did as imitation, the freest kind of translation, in which the translator ignores his subject's words and sense and merely "sets him as a pattern, to write as he supposes that author would have done, had he lived in our age and our country."

Between these two possibilities, Dryden described one which he called paraphrase, or "translation with latitude, where the author is kept in view by the translator, so as never to be lost, but his words are not so strictly followed as his sense, and that too is permitted to be amplified, but not altered."

The present version is a measured paraphrase. I have attempted to keep Catullus always in sight, and I have written in measures that try to imitate those in which he wrote. His measures were quantitative; that is to say, they were based on a system in which syllables were described as either absolutely long or short; most measured verse today in English is qualitative, based on a system in which syllables are described as relatively stressed or unstressed. No one has ever gotten a system based on length of syllable to work well in English, but it is not difficult to create measures, based on stress rather than length of syllable, that are able to give the modern reader some sense of the importance that meter had in its original.

There is at present a kind of inertial received wisdom which holds that such matters are unimportant, that paying attention to them actually interferes with the work of translation. But if your poet is a high-wire walker, you are not going to be able to convey the excitement he generates by tiptoeing along a piece of string stretched out on the floor. I have been as strict within my forms as I was able to, since Catullus worked within strict forms; he had to make choices, and it seems to me that only a translator who accepts restrictions on his freedom like those embraced by his original will be able to convey the nature of those choices.

A NOTE ON THE TEXT

For the most part I have relied on E. T. Merrill's durable edition, but am grateful to be able to acknowledge my indebtedness to the more recent editions of C. J. Fordyce and Kenneth Quinn. I have adopted Bergk's emendation of poem 1, l. 9 (*qualecumque quidem est, patroni ut ergo* for *qualecumque; quod o patrona virgo*) as well as his suggestion that fragments 2b and 14b are, reversed in order, the divorced halves of a single poem, here included as 1b. In poem 41, l. 1, I have accepted Pleitner's *amens illa* for *Ameana*. I have followed the traditional numbering of the poems, which accounts for the hiatus between poems 17 and 21, a gap at one time occupied by three doubtful interpolations generally regarded as spurious by modern editors.

THE POEMS OF

CATULLUS

To whom will I give this sophisticated,
abrasively accomplished new collection?
To you, Cornelius! You had the habit
of making much of my poetic little,
when you, the first in Italy, were boldly
unfolding all past ages in three volumes,
a monument of scholarship & labor!
And so it's yours; I hand this slim book over, *immortality*
such as it is—for the sake of its patron
may it survive a century or better.

If any of you happen to be future
readers of these trivial indecencies
& find that you can touch us without bristling,
I'd be as pleased with that as Atalanta
was, in the story, with the golden apple
that freed her of virginity's restrictions.

Sparrow, you darling pet of my beloved,
which she caresses, presses to her body
or teases with the tip of one sly finger
until you peck at it in tiny outrage!
—for there are times when my desired, shining
lady is moved to turn to you for comfort,
to find (as I imagine) ease for ardor,
solace, a little respite from her sorrow—
if I could only play with you as she does,
and be relieved of my tormenting passion!

Cry out lamenting, Venuses & Cupids,
and mortal men endowed with Love's refinement:
the sparrow of my lady lives no longer!
Sparrow, the darling pet of my beloved,
that was more precious to her than her eyes were;
it was her little honey, and it knew her
as well as any girl knows her own mother;
it would not ever leave my lady's bosom
but leapt up, fluttering from yon to hither,
chirruping always only to its mistress.
It now flits off on its way, goes, gloom-laden
down to where—word is—there is no returning.
Damn you, damned shades of Orcus that devour
all mortal loveliness, for such a lovely
sparrow it was you've stolen from my keeping!
O hideous deed! O poor little sparrow!
It's your great fault that my lady goes weeping,
reddening, ruining her eyes from sorrow.

Closer, friends: this little yacht you see before you
says that in her day no ship afloat was swifter,
no craft cut water whose wake she wasn't able
to leave behind, no matter whether her oarblades
drove her along or she relied on her canvas!
The shoreline of the blustery Adriatic
won't deny it, nor will the Cycladic Islands,
nor glamourous Rhodes, no—not even the wild Thracian
sea of Marmora, nor the grim gulf of Pontus,
where in the past our future yacht resided
as a green forest on the heights of Cytorus,
and where she learned to lisp in leafy syllables.
Pontic Amastris, Cytorus of the boxwood,
this little beanpod says that her past & present
are well known to you; she's certain you remember
how life began for her, perched atop your summit,
and how she first dipped her new oars into your waters,
leaving you on her maiden voyage through stormy
seas with her master, heading straight as an arrow
no matter whether the wind was holding steady
from port or starboard or from both sides together.
Nor was it ever necessary to offer
vows to the gods because of her performance
on the open seas or these more tranquil waters.
Now her career is ended, and in her old age
retiring, she dedicates herself to you two,
Castor the twin & the twin brother of Castor.

Lesbia, let us live only for loving,
and let us value at a single penny
all the loose flap of senile busybodies!
Suns when they set are capable of rising,
but at the setting of our own brief light
night is one sleep from which we never waken.
Give me a thousand kisses, then a hundred,
another thousand next, another hundred,
a thousand without pause & then a hundred,
until when we have run up our thousands
we will cry bankrupt, hiding our assets
from ourselves & any who would harm us,
knowing the volume of our trade in kisses.

Flavius, if your new infatuation
weren't some dull slut, you wouldn't keep silent—
you'd *have* to tell Catullus all about her.
I really can't imagine this hotblooded
whore you're so keen on—shame must have you tongue-tied!
You do not lie alone: even though speechless,
your little love nest is a revelation,
dripping with garlands & exotic odors,
not to mention the battered pillows scattered
around the couch gone prematurely feeble
from your incessant nighttime acrobatics!
There isn't any point to keeping quiet:
we know you're doing it—even your vanished
love-handles show how fiercely you've been fucking!
So whatever you have, whether nice or nasty,
tell us—for I would raise you and your passion
right up to heaven with my clever verses.

· 7 ·

My Lesbia, you ask how many kisses
would be enough to satisfy, to sate me!
—As many as the sandgrains in the desert
near Cyrene, where silphium is gathered,
between the shrine of Jupiter the sultry
& the venerable sepulchre of Battus!
—As many as the stars in the tacit night
that watch as furtive lovers lie embracing:
only to kiss you with that many kisses
would satisfy, could sate your mad Catullus!
A sum to thwart the reckoning of gossips
& baffle the spell-casting tongues of envy.

Wretched Catullus! You have to stop this nonsense,
admit that what you see has ended is over!
Once there were days which shone for you with rare brightness,
when you would follow wherever your lady led you,
the one we once loved as we will love no other;
there was no end in those days to our pleasures,
when what you wished for was what she also wanted.
Yes, there were days which shone for you with rare brightness.
Now she no longer wishes; you mustn't want it,
you've got to stop chasing her now—cut your losses,
harden your heart & hold out firmly against her.
Goodbye now, lady. Catullus' heart is hardened,
he will not look to you nor call against your wishes—
how you'll regret it when nobody comes calling!
So much for you, bitch—your life is all behind you!
Now who will come to see you, thinking you lovely?
Whom will you love now, and whom will you belong to?
Whom will you kiss? And whose lips will you nibble?
But *you*, Catullus! *You* must hold out now, firmly!

Veranius, more dear to me than any
300,000 of my many dear friends,
have you returned to your family's altar,
your grateful brothers & your aged mother?
You *have* returned! What a blessing this news is!
I'll see you safe & sound at home, describing
what went on in Spain, the rare tribes & places,
as only you can do it—I'll embrace you,
I'll press your darling mouth & eyes with kisses!
Among those men who have been blessed by fortune,
who is more pleased than I, more beatific?

Ran into Varus over at the forum,
just killing time. We went to see his girlfriend,
who struck me right away as—well, a hooker,
bur fairly clever & not unattractive.
While we were at her place the conversation
turned, among other things, to what the news was
out of Bithynia, how it had gone there,
had I made any money from the province.
I told them what the score was: natives nothing,
nothing for governors or their lieutenants:
no one comes back from there rolling in money—
and that cornholing bastard we went out with
just didn't give a damn about our pockets!
"But surely," they said, "surely you were able
to buy yourself some slaves to use as coolies?
Aren't they bred there?"
                         I wanted to impress her,
to make her think that I was something special:
"Poor as the province was I got assigned to,"
I told them both, "that doesn't mean I couldn't
buy a fine team of eight upstanding porters."
Needless to say, I nowhere own a single
slave who'd even be capable of hoisting
the whacked-off leg of some old beggar's pallet.
True sluttishness will out. The harlot begged me,
"Catullus, sweetie, lend 'em for an hour,
I wan'na worship at Serapis' temple."
"Hold on," I told her, "when I said that *I* owned
them, that I *owned* those slaves, I wasn't thinking—

a dear friend of mine, Gaius, Gaius Cinna,
he owns them, but although they're his, he lets me
take them as though they were my own," I told her.
"But really, there are some things I just *can't* take;
tedious, tasteless & insistent bitches
with which you can't be off your guard one minute!"

Aurelius & Furius, true comrades,
whether Catullus penetrates to where in
outermost India booms the eastern ocean's
  wonderful thunder;

whether he stops with Arabs or Hyrcani,
Parthian bowmen or nomadic Sagae;
or goes to Egypt, which the Nile so richly
  dyes, overflowing;

even if he should scale the lofty Alps, or
summon to mind the mightiness of Caesar
viewing the Gallic Rhine, the dreadful Britons
  at the world's far end—

you're both prepared to share in my adventures,
and any others which the gods may send me.
Back to my girl then, carry her this bitter
  message, these spare words:

May she have joy & profit from her cocksmen,
go down embracing hundreds all together,
never with love, but without interruption
  wringing their balls dry;

nor look to my affection as she used to,
for she has left it broken, like a flower
at the edge of a field after the plowshare
  brushes it, passing.

· 12 ·

It's sinister, Asinius—your practice
of lifting our unprotected napkins
while we're all deep in wine & conversation!
You're crazy if you think you're being clever:
what could be shabbier or less attractive?
But don't take my word—go & ask your brother,
for Pollio would gladly spend a fortune
to keep it quiet; that boy is a master
of every grace that's charming & delightful.
So either send me back my linen napkin
or else expect three hundred savage verses—
I'm not upset because it was expensive,
but it's a gift which calls to mind a friendship:
Veranius & my Fabullus sent it
all the way back from Spain for me, a present
which I must therefore cherish as I cherish
my dear Fabullus & Veraniolus.

You will dine well with me, my dear Fabullus,
in a few days or so, the gods permitting.
—Provided you provide the many-splendored
feast, and invite your fair-complected lady,
your wine, your salt & all the entertainment!
Which is to say, my dear, if you bring dinner
you will dine well, for these days your Catullus
finds that his purse is only full of cobwebs.
But in return, you'll have from me Love's Essence,
—or what (if anything) is more delicious:
I'll let you sniff a certain charming fragrance
which Venuses & Cupids gave my lady;
one whiff of it, Fabullus, and you'll beg the
gods to transform you into nose, completely!

Calvus, you darling, if I didn't love you
more than my own eyes, this gift would make me
hate you as much as Vatinius hates you!
What did I say or do to give you reason
for wasting me with such outrageous poets?
May all the gods goddam whichever client
sent you this swarm of miserable sinners!
But if—as I suspect—this rare, exquisite
work is your fee from Sulla the schoolmaster,
then it's another story: I'm delighted
to learn that you got anything from *that* one!
God, what a dreadful lot of holy rubbish!
What an awful book! And you just *had* to send it
over at once to murder your Catullus
at the best of all times, the Saturnalia!
How clever of you! But it isn't finished:
if morning ever comes, I'll run & gather
all sorts of poison from the bins of bookstalls:
men like Suffenus, Caesius, Aquinus,
abominations fit for retribution!
—And as for you, damned nuisances, you're banished;
limp back on wretched feet to your creators,
the worst of poets & the age's penance!

My soul is yours, in trust with my beloved,
Aurelius. I ask a modest favor:
if you have ever in your heart been anxious
to keep a lover faithful & unworldly,
see that my darling doesn't get in trouble.
I'm not afraid of strangers getting at him,
men in the streets preoccupied with business,
rushing about too madly for seductions:
it's you I really fear—you & your penis,
which means no good to boys both nice & naughty!
Do what you want to anyone you want to
as often as you wish, when you're out cruising:
spare me one only—that's a modest favor.
But if infatuation's raging madness
urges you on to any monkey business,
ah! how I dread the end you'll come to, tortured
like an adulterer before the people:
feet bound together, nether door propped open
with a ripe bunch of radishes & mullets.

I'll fuck the pair of you as you prefer it,
oral Aurelius, anal Furius,
who read my verses but misread their author:
you think that *I'm* effeminate, since *they* are!
Purity's proper in the godly poet,
but it's unnecessary in his verses,
which really should be saucy & seductive,
even salacious in a girlish manner
and capable of generating passion
not just in boys, but in old men who've noticed
getting a hard-on has been getting harder!
But you, because my poems beg for kisses,
thousands of kisses, you think I'm a fairy!
I'll fuck the pair of you as you prefer it.

O poor Verona, you who wish a new bridge for the festive
dances you'd hold if you weren't afraid of the ill-fitting
legs of your old one, that sagging pile of secondhand lumber
just about ready to flop in the muck surging around it—
may you get a new bridge, just as strong as you could desire,
one that can handle even the rites of Salisubsalis,
if only you'll do me this one, hugely amusing favor:
I want a certain townsman of mine to go hurtling headlong
off of your bridge & summersault wildly into the mire,
and please—let it be right at that very spot where the reeking
gunk of that whole malodorous marsh is blackest & deepest!
The man's an absolute ass—even a two-year-old baby
asleep in the tremulous arms of his father is brighter:
you see, he's married a mere child, a girl barely pubescent,
and a girl like that, friskier than a capering kidling,
ought to be guarded more closely than grapes at their ripest.
But does he watch her? not him: he lets her play as she pleases:
that boring, complacent old cuckold lies like an alder
dumped in a ditch, hamstrung by a sharp Ligurian hatchet—
insensate cornute, unconscious of what his wife's doing!
So great a stupor has this one that he sees & hears nothing,
and doesn't know what he is, or whether he is—or he isn't!
Now *he's* the one that I want to see plunge from your old bridge
      headfirst:
the sudden shock might help him shake off his leaden
      obtuseness,
and leave his spineless spirit to sink behind in the mire,
as a mule caught in the muck will lose its iron-shod footgear.

Aurelius, you father of starvations,
not just of these afflicting us at present,
but those as well of past & future ages,
you'd like to slip it into my beloved!
—No secret how you cling beside him, camping
outrageously, exploring all approaches.
Well, it won't work. You'll see how I'll defile you,
if you continue with this monkey business!
I wouldn't say a word, were you a fat man,
but how can I endure my boy enduring
lessons in drought & famine from the Master?
So give it up now, save your reputation,
or watch out for a savage fucking over!

Varus, you know Suffenus as well as any;
the man is charming, witty, sophisticated—
nevertheless, he's written reams of bad verses.
I'm sure he must have churned out more than ten thousand,
and not just jotted down on scraps of papyrus,
as we do—no, they're copied out on good new rolls
wound up on ivory, with red parchment wrappers,
lead-ruled, smoothed with pumice: what a grand production!
And when you *read* his stuff, this darling man, our
sophisticated Suffenus seems a perfect
goatsucker, miles away from his urbane brilliance.
Who can explain this? A man brighter than diamonds
or what (if anything) is even more polished,
becomes less clever than the least clever rustic
when he turns to verse. At the same time, he's never
more beatific than when he's busy writing—
pleased and even astounded by his own talent.
Conceited? Yes, but show me a man who isn't:
someone who doesn't seem like Suffenus in something.
A glaring fault? It must be somebody else's:
I carry mine in my backpack & ignore them.

You've got no servant, Furius, no money,
no bedbug, no spider spinning by no fire—
you've got a father though, and a stepmother
whose teeth can grind the toughest stone to gravel!
—It's beautiful, the life you lead with these two,
your father & your father's withered woman.
No wonder, for the three of you are thriving,
your sound digestions undisturbed by worry:
no fear of fires, of collapsing buildings,
the knives of thieves, the venom of assassins,
or any other routine urban perils.
Your constitutions are as dry as horn is,
or what (if anything) is even drier,
thanks to your diet & your outdoor lifestyle.
Remarkable, the way you go on living
with neither sweat nor spittle—thus, no hacking
coughs, no runny noses. To these *nice* touches,
add one last refinement: an asshole gleaming
with all the radiance of polished silver!
Ten times a year or less it opens, chucking
a pellet harder than a bean or pebble—
and each of them so nicely inoffensive,
that if you crumble one between your fingers
it leaves no stain! O Furius, you prosper!
Don't throw away all this, don't say it's nothing!
You need a hundred thousand? No, stop asking:
you have your fortune—but it can't be counted!

O you who are the perfect budding flower
of all Juventians—not just of these now,
but those as well of past & future ages,
I'd sooner have you give the wealth of Midas
to one who has no servant & no money
than have you give yourself to his embraces.
"Why not?" you ask me, "isn't he darling?"

Yes,

but Darling has no servant & no money.
Throw out my words, discount them if you want to,
but still he has no servant & no money.

Thallus, you fairy far far softer than the fur of bunny
or the down of goose or the fine fuzz of a fuzzy earlobe
or an old man's limp dick or the dusty cobwebs that it's hung
   with—
Thallus, who sweeps up our belongings like a crazed cyclone
when the goddess of sloth reveals that his victims are nodding—
send them *all* back to me: the cloak you've lately pounced upon &
my Spanish napkins & my notebooks full of Eastern sketches
which you (dumb booby) openly display—as family heirlooms!
Peel my possessions from your gummy fingers & remit them,
lest your smooth fanny & your precious mollycoddled hands be
scribbled upon, covered with rude graffiti by the whip's lash
and you yourself be tossed & blown about like a too tiny
cabin cruiser caught on the open seas in heavy weather.

Your little villa, Furius: it faces
no danger from the south wind or the west wind,
the cruel north wind or the east wind either:
it merely faces imminent foreclosure,
a wicked blow & terribly unhealthy.

Waiter, Falernian! That fine old wine, boy:
pour me another bowl & make it stronger.
—Postumia, the mistress of these revels,
loaded as the vines are, she's laid the law down:
go elsewhere, water. Go to where you're wanted,
spoiler of wine, go—pass your sober days with
sober people. Up Bacchus, undiluted.

Comrades of Piso, retinue of paupers
with your belongings all bound up in bindles,
noble Veranius, my *dear* Fabullus,
how is it going? Haven't you both had it,
enduring frost & famine with that wastrel?
—Do your accounts show such accumulated
losses as I had, in my praetor's service?
This was the profit set down in my ledger:
"Yet once again, O Memmius, your pliant
member, eased *all* the way in, leaves me speechless."
But I can see how similar your case is,
how big a prick it is by which you're shafted!
—That's what you get for chasing after rich friends!
May all the gods & goddesses goddamn you,
unworthy heirs of Romulus & Remus.

Who could stand by, patiently watching this happen,
but someone shameless—a greedy, reckless gambler?
Shall Mamurra have what Gaul beyond the mountains
had before him—*and* the wealth of distant Britain?
You faggot, Romulus! Can you bear to watch this?
—popping with pride now, he struts off, promenading
through all the best bedrooms like a new Adonis
or a snowy dove cock, Aphrodite's darling!
You, faggot Romulus! Can you bear to watch this?
Then you *are* shameless—a greedy, reckless gambler!
Was it on his account, O my peerless leader,
that you set out to make war on distant Britain?
—so that this detumescent prick on your payroll
could waste another twenty or thirty million?
If that isn't a lefthanded handout, what is?
Is there no end at all to his plowing & swilling?
After he spent the money left by his father,
he went through the loot from your campaign in Pontus,
and then the gold won on your Spanish adventure:
now we must fear the same fate for Gaul & Britain!
Why do you nourish this pest? What is he good for,
but to devour fortune after great fortune?
Was it for his sake that you brought total ruin
upon us all, O Caesar—you & your Pompey?

You're false, Alfenus, false to those friends who foolishly trusted
   you—
have you no pity now for the one you once called your beloved?
Worse, far worse—for now you're even willing to cheat & betray
   me!
The gods in heaven are angered by the impious acts of bad men;
you treat them lightly, leaving me to sink in my troubles.
Tell me, Alfenus, what are men to do? Whom can they put faith
   in?
Don't you remember how you insisted that I could count on you,
and led me into love with your lying promises of safety?
Now you back off from all of those promises—your words &
   deeds are
scattered completely, given over to the wind & misty vapors.
Though you've forgotten, the gods remember, Good Faith
   remembers and
shortly will see you punished for the cruel way that you've
   treated me.

· 31 ·

None of the other islands & peninsulas
which Neptune floats on sheets of untroubled water
or on the desolate face of the vast ocean
please me, delight me, dear Sirmio, as you do!
I still can't believe I've gotten back here safely
from Thynia, Bithynia—and stand before you!
What could be better? Every care dissolving,
shedding the burden of an exhausting journey,
back home among the gods of our own household
we find at last the couch, the rest we desired!
This alone repays us for our long labors.
How are you, sexy Sirmio! Rejoice with your master,
and you too, bubbling lake of Lydian waters—
loose every last chortle of your locked-up laughter!

I beg of you, my sweet, my Ipsitilla,
my darling, my sophisticated beauty,
summon me to a midday assignation;
and, if you're willing, do me one big favor:
don't let another client shoot the door bolt,
and don't decide to suddenly go cruising,
but stay at home & get yourself all ready
for nine—yes, nine—successive copulations!
Honestly, if you want it, give the order:
I've eaten, and I'm sated, supinated!
My prick is poking through my cloak & tunic.

O best of all who work the bathhouse rackets,
Vibennius & Son, that letching asshole!
(for father's hand is utterly rapacious
& his boy's fanny is no less voracious)
why don't you both go straight to hell together,
now that the father's thefts are common knowledge,
and you, son, have no hope of finding buyers
who'll pay a penny for such hairy buttocks.

We are in Diana's keeping,
boys & girls who are unmarried;
let us sing now of Diana,
    sing, unmarried girls & boys.

Latona's child, great daughter of
Jove who is greatest in heaven,
Goddess whose mother bore Thee by an
    olive tree upon Delos

to be the mistress of mountains
& of deep, greenwooded forests,
of the hidden, wild back country
    & the resonant rivers:

women who cry out in labor
call upon Thee as lightbearing
Juno, but Thou art Trivia
    too, and counterfeit Luna.

In monthly parts Thou measurest
Thy journey through the year's cycle,
filling the sheds of the farmer
    with a harvest of ripe grain.

Under whichever name honors
Thee most, be pleased with our worship;
now, as before, keep the Romans
    safe in Thy benevolence.

Go, poem, pay a call on Caecilius,
my friend the master of erotic verses:
tell him to leave his lakefront place at Comum
& spend a little time here at Verona,
for I have certain weighty cogitations
to deliver—words from a friend of ours!
—Wherefore, if he is wise, he'll get the lead out,
although a thousand times his peerless lady
should seize him, fling her arms about his neck, and
beg him to linger in her soft embraces.
That girl is crazy for him; if the story
I've heard is true, she perishes of passion:
for ever since she first read his unfinished
poem, his epic *Mistress of Dindymus*,
flames have been feeding on her deepest marrow.
Lady more artful than the Sapphic Muse is,
I feel for you! It really is exquisite,
his almost finished poem on Cybele.

Asswiper poems Volusius made, you
shat-on sheets can help my girl keep her promise:
she swore to holy Venus & to Cupid
that if we two could get it back together
and I'd stop shooting off my sharp iambics,
she'd gather from the wretchedest of poets
a proper sacrifice for gimpy Vulcan:
lamefooted verse to burn with blighted branches.
She thought it all too clever, and imagined
the gods would find her little vow amusing.
Wherefore, O Venus, born of skyblue waters,
who dwellest on Idalium, at Urii,
at Ancon & at reed-exporting Cnidus,
at Amathus, at Golgi, at the seaport
of Durrachium on the Adriatic,
accept these worthy offerings as payment,
if my astuteness charms you to approval.
And now it's time to feed you to the fire,
boggle of boondockish, clodkicker verses,
asswiper poems. Volusius made you.

Bawdyhouse barroom, nine pillars past the temple
of Castor & Pollux! And you who get drunk there!
—Can you believe that you're the world's only lovers,
the only ones licensed to offer the ladies
a proper screwing? The rest of us are just goats?
You hundred dullards sitting in a row! Or is it
two hundred, dullards? Do you think that I wouldn't
dare to fuck over the lot of you as you sit there?
Think what you wish to think, dullards—but I'll scribble
cocks & cunts all over the front of your building!
For here the girl who has fled from my embraces,
she who was loved as no one else ever will be,
for whom I fought so many terrible battles,
she sits her down here. And here her worthy lovers
come, all of them—and in unworthy addition,
all of her common crew of cocksmen & lechers;
and foremost among this mob of longhaired dandies
art thou, Egnatius, son of coneyed Iberia,
whose untrimmed beard, and teeth polished in the Spanish
manner—with urine—mark as distinguished. Very.

By Hercules, it's hard for your Catullus,
hard, Cornificius: it is a labor,
and it grows greater every day & hour!
—But you, when nothing could have been less trouble,
did you write anything to give me comfort?
I'm growing angry! This, from my beloved?
Send on a line or two in consolation,
sadder than all the tears of Simonides.

Because he's so proud of his white teeth, Egnatius
goes about grinning! If he comes to the courtroom
while the defendant's lawyer is plucking our heartstrings,
there he is, grinning! Next to the mother mourning
her only son dead on the funeral pyre,
there he is, grinning his grin for all occasions,
no matter where or when. It is a strange sickness,
as inelegant, I feel, as it's unclever.
And so—my fine Egnatius—I must correct you:
if you were Roman, or Sabine, or Tiburtine,
were you an Umbrian, or an Etruscan,
or a Lanuvian, all swart & toothy,
or a Transpadane, to mention my own people,
or anyone at all who brushed his teeth nicely,
I still wouldn't want to see you always grinning,
for nothing is more inept than inept laughter.
But you're a Spaniard; and it's the Spanish custom
to brush your teeth & reddish gums every morning
with the foul water that you've made in the nighttime!
And so your gleaming teeth only serve to remind us
what a great lot of piss you've recently swallowed.

Poor little Ravidus! What madness drives you
on to be shafted by my sharp iambics?
What god offended by a faulty prayer
makes you provoke this quarrel so insanely?
—Or are you only eager to be noticed,
a famous man, no matter what the cost is?
You will be! Since you choose to love my darling,
and for a great while after you'll repent it.

This crazy girl, so thoroughly fucked over,
demands that I should pay her her ten thousand!
That girl with the repulsive nose, the worthless
whore of the bankrupt Formian, Mamurra!
Now you—the girl's relations—you're in charge here,
you'd better call her friends & get the doctors:
she isn't well, this girl—and never bothers
to pause before a mirror for reflection.

Up now, iambics—get yourselves together,
all of you everywhere, however many!
—A flaming slut imagines that she'll mock me,
and now refuses to return the tablets
I write you verses down on—can you bear it?
Let's follow her & force her to return them.
Who're you after? *Her*—that one you see there,
shaking her ass & mouthing like a mimic,
the rabid bitch with the repulsive grimace!
Surround her now & force her to return them:
"You wretched slut you give us back the tablets,
give us the tablets back you wretched slut you!"
Doesn't that bother you? You filth, you flophouse,
you drain on even *my* profound invective!
—We mustn't think we've gotten satisfaction:
if nothing else, at least we can embarrass
the bitch & give her cheeks a little color.
Cry out once more, in unison & louder:
"You wretched slut you give us back the tablets,
give us the tablets back you wretched slut you!"
We're getting nowhere. Nothing seems to move her.
Maybe we ought to try another tactic
and see if it won't work a little better:
"Maiden most modest, give us back the tablets."

Greetings to you, girl of the nose not tiny,
the feet not pretty, eyes not darkly-shadowed,
stubby fat fingers, mouth forever spraying
language that shows us your lack of refinement,
whore of that bankrupt wastrel from Formiae!
Is it your beauty they praise in the province?
Do they compare you to our Lesbia?
Mindless, this age. And insensitive, really.

· 44 ·

Dear Sabine shanty—or dear Tiburtine villa
(for those who love Catullus will claim you're in Tibur,
while those whose thing it is to rile me will gamble
any amount at any odds you're just Sabine)
but whether you're Sabine or—indeed—Tiburtine,
I really enjoyed myself at your suburban
hideaway, while I recovered from the chest cold
my belly gave me as a righteous penance
for chasing all over after sumptuous dinners.
Sestius asked me out—and I was so eager,
I read the venomous & pestilential
oration he made opposing Antius!
Came down with chills at once. My persistent coughing
finally drove me from town to your embraces,
where I was cured by rest & the broth of nettles!
Wholly recovered, I thank you for not having
taken advantage of a poor wretched sinner:
and if I ever again touch the Infected
Works of Sestius, may I die of pneumonia!
And not only me, no—but Sestius also,
whose invitations put one in mortal danger.

Septimius, with his beloved Acme
curled on his lap, moans, "Acme, dear, my darling,
unless I love you, Love, unto perdition,
now & forever after, with a frenzy
as fierce as any fabled frenzied lover's,
may I be savaged by a green-eyed lion,
in Libya or India the torrid!"
(As Cupid heard, he sneezed in approbation,
rapidly first on one side then the other.)
—But Acme coyly tilted back her head, and
covered her lover's swimming eyes with kisses
fresh from her mouth as luscious as a berry:
"Septimius," she said, "my life, my darling,
forever may we both serve this one master,
as now I swear by Love's consuming fire—
from which I suffer rather more than you do."
(As Cupid heard, he sneezed in approbation,
rapidly first on one side then the other.)
They start from so fortuitous an omen,
their loving & beloved souls entangled:
Septimius would rather have his Acme
than a great heap of Syrias & Britains.
And in Septimius, his faithful Acme
finds nothing less than total satisfaction!
Who's ever witnessed a more beatific
couple, or known sweet Venus more auspicious?

Spring fetches back the days of warming weather,
the equinoctial bluster of the heavens
is silenced by the Zephyr's tender breezes.
It's time to leave the plains of Troy, Catullus,
and the rich, sweltering fields of Nicaea:
those glamourous Aegean cities beckon!
My mind is really anxious to be going,
my feet are dancing with anticipation!
So it's good-by now to those dear companions
who set out from a distant home together,
whom varied roads now carry back diversely.

Well, if it isn't Pestilence & Famine,
sinister hirelings of mobster Piso!
Has that licentious prick picked you two over
my dear Fabullus & Veraniolus?
And does he feed you lavishly at banquets
while it's still light out? While my poor companions
lurk at the crossroads, looking for some action?

Juventius, if I could play at kissing
your honeyed eyes as often as I wished to,
300,000 games would not exhaust me;
never could I be satisfied or sated,
although the total of our osculations
were greater than the ears of grain at harvest.

Most eloquent of all the past & present
offspring of Romulus, O Marcus Tully,
—and of all those to come in future ages!
You've won the gratitude of your Catullus,
who is most certainly the worst of poets;
as certainly the very worst of poets
as you are—certainly—the best of lawyers.

Just yesterday, Licinius, at leisure,
we played around for hours with my tablets
writing erotic verse as we'd agreed to,
each of us taking turns at improvising
line after line in meter after meter,
adjuncts to wine & witty conversation.
And when I left you, I was so on fire
with all your brilliant & ironic humor
that after dinner I was still excited,
and sleep refused to touch my eyes with quiet.
In bed & totally unstrung by passion,
tossing in agony, I prayed for sunrise,
when I could be with you in conversation.
But when my limbs, exhausted by their labor,
lay on the bed in nearly fatal stillness,
I made this poem for you, my beloved,
so you could take the measure of my sorrow.
I beg you to be kind to my petition,
darling, for if you aren't, if you're cruel,
them Nemesis will turn on you in outrage.
Don't rile her up, please—she's a bitch, that goddess.

To me that man seems like a god in heaven,
seems—may I say it?—greater than all gods are,
who sits by you & without interruption
            watches you, listens

to your light laughter, which casts such confusion
onto my senses, Lesbia, that when I
gaze at you merely, all of my well-chosen
            words are forgotten

as my tongue thickens & a subtle fire
runs through my body while my ears are deafened
by their own ringing & at once my eyes are
            covered in darkness!

Leisure, Catullus. More than just a nuisance,
leisure: you riot, overmuch enthusing.
Fabulous cities & their sometime kings have
            died of such leisure.

Catullus, what keeps you from killing yourself? No good reason.
That tumor Nonius sits in the chair of a magistrate,
and lying Vatinius swears by his imminent consulship.
Catullus, what keeps you from killing yourself? No good reason.

The courthouse mobscene: I led all the laughter
just now, when someone who had heard my Calvus
neatly expose Vatinius the gangster
threw up his hands & cried in admiration,
"Great gods, this little pecker's sure persuasive!"

Otho stores his puny wit in a thimble

. . . .

Hirrus, you ought to wash your legs more often;
pungent & penetrating farts from Libo

. . . .

those things at least, I should have thought, would anger
you & Fulficius, that senile cocksman

. . . .

once more you will be outraged by my iambs,
which don't deserve it, O my peerless leader

Tell us, if it isn't too much trouble,
where it is that you've been lurking lately.
We've looked all over for you—at the racetrack,
at the Circus, in the Forum's bookstalls,
the sacred temple of great Jupiter!
I went as far as Pompey's portico,
questioning every hooker who approached me:
what a lot of innocent expressions!
Unconvinced, I finally exploded,
"Give me Camerius, you bargain baggage!"
One answered me with a complete disclosure:
"He's hiding here, between my blushing titties. . . ."
You think I'm Hercules? I'm not. Even
if I were changed into the Cretan Giant,
and had the wings of Pegasus for soaring,
and were as fast as Perseus or Ladas,
or the white horses of the Thracian King;
add all flying fowl of every feather,
and have the winds rush in from every quarter;
order them all, Camerius, to aid me
and still I'd be worn down to a frazzle,
suffer fainting spells & palpitations,
and God knows what, my friend, from chasing you!
It really isn't nice to be so distant.
Come on now, tell us where we can reach you,
put an end to this absurd deception!
Are your little blondes holding you captive?
If you remain obstinately tongue-tied,

the rewards of love will all escape you:
Venus likes nothing more than juicy gossip.
But if you must, keep it from the others,
so long as I can share your little secret!

· 56 ·

Cato, it was absurd, just too amusing,
fit for your ears & fit to make you cackle!
You'll laugh if you love your Catullus, Cato:
it was absurd & really *too* amusing!
Just now I came across a young boy swiving
his girlfriend, and—don't take offense now, Venus!
I pinned him to his business with my skewer.

How well these two bad fairies fit together,
this queenly couple, Caesar & Mamurra!
—No wonder, for they're like as two like smutches
(one is from Rome, a Formian the other)
sunk in too deeply to be gotten rid of:
a pair of twins with all the same diseases,
they lie entangled on one couch to scribble,
adulterers both, equally voracious,
and with nymphetoleptic dispositions:
how well these two bad fairies fit together!

Lesbia, Caelius—yes, our darling,
yes, *Lesbia*, the Lesbia Catullus
once loved uniquely, more than any other!
—now on streetcorners & in wretched alleys
she shucks the offspring of greathearted Remus.

RUFA THE BOLOGNESE WIFE OF MENENIUS
SUCKS RUFULUS COCK
           Often, in some cheap graveyard
you will have seen her snatch a loaf as it tumbles
from the fiery logs of the funeral pyre,
while the half-shaven corpse-burner thwacks away at her
    backside.

Either a lioness from Libya's mountains
or Scylla barking from her terrible bitch-womb
gave birth to you, so foul & so hard your heart is:
the great contempt you show as I lie here dying
with not a word from you! Such a beastly coldness.

You who abide on Helicon,
son of Urania, god who
hastens the tender bride to her
bridegroom, *O Hymenaee Hymen,*
5   *O Hymen Hymenaee,*

cover your head with a garland
of fragrant marjoram flowers,
put on your flame-colored mantle,
come merrily, wearing yellow
10   slippers on your snowy feet!

Waking on this festive morning,
chanting the poems of marriage
in a sweetly tremulant voice,
pound the earth under your feet and
15   whirl the pine torch in your hand,

for today Manlius marries
Vinia, who is as lovely
as was Idalian Venus
when Paris made his decision:
20   she goes with good auspices,

as dear as Lydian myrtle
is to the nymphs of the forest!
They love their flowery plaything,
brilliant with sprigs of white blossoms,
25   and feed it on dewdrops.

Come to us, come to us quickly!
Set about leaving your shelter,
your cave on Helicon, cooled by
water that falls from the fountain
    of the nymph Aganippe.   30

Call to her home its new mistress,
eager to be with her husband;
fasten her heart with affection
as trailing ivy will fasten
    around the base of a tree.   35

And you too, O maids in waiting,
for whom a day just like this one
approaches, cry out in measure,
sing it: *O Hymenaee Hymen,*
    O Hymen Hymenaee,   40

so he will come here with greater
eagerness, hearing us summon
him to his duties, this herald
of lawful Venus, this god who
    seals our lawful passions.   45

What god more worthily called on
by those whose love is requited?
Whom shall men worship more in all
heaven? *O Hymenaee Hymen,*
    O Hymen Hymenaee.   50

The trembling father invokes you;
for your sake, virgins loosen the
bindings that gather their dresses;
eager, the nervous young bridegroom
55   jumps when he hears your music!

You give the budding girl over
to the hands of her hot husband,
take her away from her mother's
bosom. *O Hymenaee Hymen,*
60   *O Hymen Hymenaee.*

Without you, Venus may give no
pleasure which one might approve of
as proper; yet she is able,
when you are willing: what god can
65   hope to compare with this one?

No house may have heirs without you,
nor aged parents have children
to lean on; yet they may have them,
when you are willing: what god can
70   hope to compare with this one?

A land that gave you no worship
would have no young men defending
its borders; yet it may have them
when you are willing: what god can
75   hope to compare with this one?

Throw back the doorbolt, the bride is
approaching! See how the torches
shake out their flamboyant tresses!

. . . .

      80

    . . . .
    . . . . she
lingers, becomingly modest;
and looking back to her childhood,
    weeps at having to leave it.   85

Let's have no more of these tears, Au-
runculeia; there's no danger
that any woman more lovely
has ever seen daylight rising
    brightly out of the ocean.   90

You're like the hyacinth standing
alone in a garden of varied
bright flowers, owned by a rich man!
Day passes while you're delaying:
    come out & join us, virgin.   95

Come out & join us now, virgin,
if it is time to: come listen
to our words—see how the torches
shake out their fiery tresses!
    Come out & join us, virgin.   100

Your husband will not go lightly
into the arms of some harlot,
shamefully risking dishonor;
he will not wish to lie sleeping
105   far from your delicate breasts,

but just as ivy twines round the
trees that are planted beside it,
he will be bound by your loving
embraces. But the day passes:
110   come out & join us, virgin.

O wedding bed to everyone

. . . .

. . . .

. . . .

115   ivory feet of the couch.

What joys will come to your master
when the night's chariot ranges,
and in the afternoons also,
what pleasures! But the day passes:
120   come out & join us, virgin.

Now boys, now! Lift high your torches,
I see the wedding veil coming—
up now & sing out in measure,
O Hymen Hymenaee io,
125   O Hymen Hymenaee.

And now it's time for the bawdy
Fescennine verses; come, pretty
boy, bribe the slaves, scatter walnuts—
everyone's heard how your master
    has dropped you—and for a girl!   130

Pretty boy, scatter the walnuts:
once you were petted & pampered,
you played with walnuts: no longer!
Now you must serve Talasio,
    pretty boy! Scatter walnuts!   135

The farmwives used to disgust you,
pretty boy—you couldn't stand them:
no longer fancied, now you are
shaved by the barber, ah! Wretched
    pretty boy! Scatter walnuts!   140

People will tell lies about you,
husband: they'll say that you haven't
left your boyfriends behind yet.
O Hymen Hymenaee io,
    O Hymen Hymenaee.   145

We know you never went cruising,
were always perfectly decent;
but now your gay life is ended.
O Hymen Hymenaee io,
    O Hymen Hymenaee.   150

Bride, you must never refuse your
husband the pleasure he asks, or
else he will ask for it elsewhere;
O Hymen Hymenaee io,
  O Hymen Hymenaee.

155

Here in the house of your husband,
great wealth & comfort await you;
be mistress here in contentment,
O Hymen Hymenaee io,
  O Hymen Hymenaee,

160

until old age is upon you,
whose white head, caught in its dozing,
seems to be nodding approval.
O Hymen Hymenaee io,
  O Hymen Hymenaee.

165

Cross the threshold in your golden
slippers for a lucky omen—
and pass through the polished doorway,
O Hymen Hymenaee io,
  O Hymen Hymenaee.

170

Look in: your husband awaits you,
lying on a couch of purple:
he is rapt with expectation.
O Hymen Hymenaee io,
  O Hymen Hymenaee.

175

That man is no less in love with
you than you are with him, even
though he keeps his passion hidden.
O Hymen Hymenaee io,
   O Hymen Hymenaee.   180

No need to lead her inside now;
let go of her smooth arm, let her
come to the couch of her husband.
O Hymen Hymenaee io,
   O Hymen Hymenaee.   185

Now you may turn down the covers,
old women, durably wedded;
make a soft place for the virgin,
O Hymen Hymenaee io,
   O Hymen Hymenaee.   190

You too may enter now, husband;
your wife has come to the bridal
chamber, and her face is shining
with the whiteness of a daisy,
   or a poppy's golden glow.   195

Husband, I've scanted you somewhat:
I swear by heaven you're no less
attractive, no, nor does Venus
neglect you. But the day passes,
   go in, stop your delaying.   200

Ah, but you weren't delaying,
you're here already; may Venus
assist you, since you so plainly
wish what you wish for, not coyly
205   hiding your most lawful love.

Anyone eager to number
the thousands of joys before you
may tally the heavenly stars
or count up the sandgrains scattered
210   on the face of Africa!

Play as you're pleased to, and shortly
show us some children! As noble
a name as yours should have offspring
continuing that patrician
215   family you represent.

I would love to see an infant
Torquatus at his mother's bosom,
reaching out with tiny fingers,
turning to smile at his father
220   sweetly, with half-parted lips.

May he resemble his father
Manlius so very closely
that the unknowing may know at
a glance that the child's expression
225   reveals his mother's virtue.

May he inherit his mother's
good name, the gift of her honor—
like the matchless reputation
drawn from Penelope's virtue
    that young Telemachus has.   230

Close the doors softly now, maidens,
this song is over. Be good to
each other, O newly wed pair:
to work now, work at the constant
    task of practicing pleasure!   235

Vesper is out: get up now, fellows, for Vesper in heaven
lifts high at long last the bright light that we've been awaiting!
It's time we were up now, time that we left the rich tables,
time for the bride to appear, and time now for the singing!
5 *Hymen, O Hymenaee, Hymen, come now, O Hymenaee.*

THE YOUNG WOMEN

See the young men there, my sisters? Get up now & face them:
surely the nightbearing star shows his Oetean fire:
it must be time now—see how the boys spring up so spryly?
They've got good reason to: their singing's hard to improve on!
10 *Hymen O Hymenaee, Hymen, come now, O Hymenaee.*

THE YOUNG MEN

Winning against them won't be easy, boys—this is no sure thing:
just look at their faces! How serious! What concentration!
Their work has paid off: what they've learned is really worth
   knowing—
and when you consider how thorough they were, it's no wonder!
15 But we just couldn't be bothered with paying attention:
practice makes perfect—it's right they should win in this contest.
Let's see if we can't get something together this minute:
soon they'll start singing and soon they'll want our responses.
Hymen O Hymenaee, Hymen, come now, O Hymenaee.

THE YOUNG WOMEN

20 Hesperus, what fire fiercer than yours crosses heaven?
—you who can tear the young child from her mother's embraces,
tear the poor terrified child from the lap of her mother
and hand the chaste daughter over to an eager young man!

Do those who sack cities carry on any more fiercely?
Hymen O Hymenaee, Hymen, come now, O Hymenaee.   25

THE YOUNG MEN

Hesperus, what fire fairer than yours shines in heaven?
—you who confirm with your flame the agreement of marriage
arranged by the husband, arranged by the parents beforehand,
but left unfinished until your bright torch has arisen.
What gift from heaven surpasses this fortunate hour?   30
Hymen O Hymenaee, Hymen, come now, O Hymenaee.

THE YOUNG WOMEN

Hesperus rising has stolen one of us, my sisters. . . .

THE YOUNG MEN

. . . for at your coming, the watchman returns to his vigil.
Night conceals thieves, but you often arrest them at daybreak,
Hesperus, returning under the name of Eous.   35
The girls all love to make up stories, falsely complaining:
what does it matter? We know what they secretly wish for.
Hymen O Hymenaee, Hymen, come now, O Hymenaee.

THE YOUNG WOMEN

Instance a flower that grows in a garden's enclosure,
unknown to cattle, untupped by the ravaging plowblade: 40
soft winds caress it, sunlight supports it, rain draws it upward;
many the young men & many the maidens who'd have it.
But when that flower's beheaded, plucked up by a sharp nail,
none of the young men & none of the maidens will have it.
Same with a virgin: while she's intact, she is cherished—   45
but when her chaste flower is lost, when her body's dishonored,
then she is no longer pleasing to boys or to girlfriends.
Hymen O Hymenaee, Hymen, come now, O Hymenaee.

Instance a vine that grows in a bare field, unwedded:
50   it never matures, it never brings forth a ripe grape;
instead, it just droops until it's all bent over double
and the tip of the vine shoot lies flat on the surface;
none of the farmers & none of the oxen will tend it.
But if that same vine is wed in its time to an elm tree,
55   many the farmers & many the oxen who'll tend it.
Same with a virgin: intact, she grows old uncared for;
but when, at the right age, she's joined to a husband in marriage,
she becomes dearer to him & less of a bother for father.
—And you, girl, don't you start fighting with such a fine
    husband:
60   that wouldn't be nice! Your father himself handed you over,
your father & mother both, and you've got to obey them.
Besides which, most of your maidenhood's owned by your
    parents:
a third belongs to your father, a third to your mother,
the last third is yours. So, don't start fighting with these two:
they've given your husband a dowry—and all of their rights in
65   this matter!
Hymen O Hymenaee, Hymen, come now, O Hymenaee.

Rapidly carried over the towering seas in his vessel,
when speed & desire led his feet to the Phrygian woodlands
Attis rushed into that forest-encircled place of the Goddess,
and there, stung by the fury of madness to utter distraction
he took a piece of sharp flint & hacked off the weight of his
     manhood.   5
Then, just as soon as she felt that her limbs were no longer virile,
while her fresh blood was still staining the soil of the earth
     beneath her,
she quickly seized in her snowy white hands the tambour you
     love so,
that tambour whose rhythms summon men to your mysteries,
     Mother;
and as her delicate fingers rattled that shell of taut oxhide,   10
she sang these words in a high-pitched, quavering voice to her
     comrades:
"Go up to her mountain forests together, O Gallae, get going,
go on together, wandering sheep of the Lady Cybele!
—you who have chosen to live as exiles in hostile surroundings,
obedient to my orders, going wherever I led you,   15
bravely enduring the truculent waters of a salt crossing;
you who've emasculated yourselves out of hatred for Venus,
now gladden the heart of your own mistress by rushing in mazes!
Empty your minds of delay & go on together, go ranging
the Phrygian home of Cybele, Phrygian woods of the Goddess,   20
where the cymbals clash together & where the tambour re-echoes,
where the Phrygian flutist hurls out the clear note from his
     curved reed,
where the frenzied Maenads toss their passionate heads crowned
     with ivy,

where wild ululations announce the form of their worship,
25 where the mad horde of the Goddess Cybele goes to be aimless,
where it is right that we meet together for intricate dancing."
As soon as Attis, that counterfeit woman, finished her singing,
her band of orgiasts flutter their tongues & cry out insanely:
their beaten tambours bellow, their cymbals clatter in answer
30 as the swift dancers go on their sinuous way to Mount Ida.
—With Attis leading them rushing to wander breathless in frenzy
the rest of them plunge into the dark forest, strung out behind
         one
who bolts like an unbroken ox, shy of the yoke's heavy burden:
racing, the Gallae surge in the path of their turbulent leader.
35 Reaching the shrine of Cybele at last, they drop in exhaustion,
too tired from their exertions even to bother with eating.
A leaden drowsiness seals the eyes they can scarcely keep open
and the great fury of madness leaves them to lie there in quiet.
But when the golden-faced Sun arose & with radiant vision
40 surveyed the clarified air, the firm earth & the formless waters,
while his fresh horses were busy scattering Night's tattered
         shadows,
Attis woke up abruptly as Slumber rushed off from beside him,
anxious to lie down in love once more with divine Pasithea.
—No longer sleeping, no longer held by his turbulent madness,
Attis turned his mind to those things which he had done to
45   himself and
calmly now, clearly, he saw where he was & what he was lacking:
struck with horror, he ran back to the windblown fringe of the
         ocean
and stood there in tears, staring out over that desolate vastness,
wretchedly mourning his loss in these words, addressed to his
         homeland:
"My country—my seed & matrix—how foolish I was to leave
50   you,

to flee my native land as a runaway slave flees his master,
and bring myself all the way here to the bleak forests of Ida,
to spend my life in the snows—in the freezing lairs of wild
      beasts,
to live as a madman haunting the lightless dens they inhabit!
What was I thinking of then? Where did I imagine I'd find you?   55
—My eyes burn with their desire to see your coast in the distance
now, while my mind is briefly free of the fury of madness.
Must I be taken from my home to dwell in these hostile forests?
Must I lose my country—my wealth—the parents & friends I
      cherish?
Must I give up the market place, the wrestling, the races,   60
to live on, ever more wretched, forever mourning my losses?
Is there a single form which my body hasn't already taken?
A woman now, once a young man, an adolescent, a boychild,
and in those days a brilliant athlete, the pride of the gamefield:
lovers thronged at my doorway, they crowded hotly on my
      threshold,   65
leaving the front of my house strewn with their colorful garlands
before I rose from my bed & went out each morning at daybreak.
Must I now be called a priestess? Must I be Cybele's handmaid?
A Maenad—a broken part of what I was—a barren creature?
Must I be forced to remain here on the snowy heights of Mount
      Ida?   70
Must I spend my life under the towering Phrygian summits
with the deer that haunts the woods & the boar that wanders the
      forests?
Now I detest what I have done to myself, and I repent it!"
And as these words rushed from the rosy lips of Attis, instantly
bringing unwelcome news to the ears of the Goddess in heaven,   75
Cybele loosens the yoke restraining her chariot's lions
and stirs to frenzy the one on the left, a killer of cattle:

"Get going," she says, "get going right now, let madness harass
      him,
let the heavy blows of madness drive him back into the forest,
80   this one with such a desire to escape from my dominion!
—Scourge your flanks with your heavy tail until they are raw &
      bloody,
make the world tremble in terror before your hideous roaring,
shake out the terrible blood-red mane on your sinewy shoulders!"
That is what dreadful Cybele said as she let loose her lion.
Unyoked, that monster arouses himself, and when he is
85   maddened
he rushes off, roaring, gouges a jagged path through the thickets
until he comes to the watery edge of the gleaming seacoast
and sees delicate Attis there by the marmoreal waters:
he bears down upon him. Possessed, Attis flees back to that wild
      forest
90   in which he spent all the rest of his life as Cybele's handmaid.

Mighty Goddess, Goddess Cybele, sacred Mistress of Dindymus,
grant that my house may be kept safe from all of your furor, my
      Lady:
drive others off into frenzy, drive others off into madness.

They say it was pine sprung from the crown of Mount Pelion
which swam clear across the perilous waters of Neptune
to the river Phasis in the realm of King Aeetes,
back in those days when the best men the Argives could muster,
eager to carry the golden fleece out of Colchis,   5
dared to go racing their swift ship over the ocean
and stirred its cerulean surface with oars made of firwood.
Athena, who keeps the towers protecting the city,
she fashioned this hurtling carriage for those young men,
she joined the timbers of pine to the curve of the firm keel.   10
That ship, the Argo, first taught the seas about sailing.
And so, when its sharp beak plowed down through the wind-
        driven waters,
when it churned the billows white by the work of its oarblades,
incredulous sea nymphs came bobbing right up to the surface,
eager to catch just a glimpse of this unheard-of marvel!   15
If ever sailors were witness to wonders, those men were,
who saw with their very own eyes the Nereids rising,
barebreasted mermaids afloat on the whiteheaded ocean.
They say it was then that Peleus burned to have Thetis,
who raised no objection to taking a mortal husband,   20
and the Father himself judged that they ought to be married.
O Heroes born in the happiest time of all ages,
the righteous offspring of gods & of mortal women,
I will not fail to celebrate you in my poem;
often I'll greet you, often your names will be mentioned,   25
and you especially, blessed beyond others in marriage,
Peleus, pillar of Thessaly, to whom the father
of heaven himself surrendered his very beloved!

Did Thetis enchant you—that loveliest of the Nereids?
30   Did Tethys give her consent to her granddaughter's marriage,
and Ocean, who cinches all of the world with his river?
    And so at last, on the appointed day of the wedding,
the people of Thessaly throng to his palace together
in celebration, fillings its chambers completely,
35   gifts in their hands, expressions of joy on their faces.
Cieros is emptied, they pour from Phthiotic Tempe,
from the houses of Crannon & out through the gates of Larissa
they come to Pharsalus & gather under its rooftops.
The land's left untilled, the backs of the oxen grow tender,
40   the curved rake no longer loosens the soil of the vineyard,
the young bull no longer breaks up the packed earth with the
        plowshare,
the dresser of vines no longer cuts back the branches of shade
        trees,
and a thin film of rust spreads over the idle equipment.
But in his opulent palace, great chambers receding
45   create a vista resplendent with glittering gold & silver;
ivory glows on the couch legs, the cups on the table gleam,
and all of that house is gay with the splendor of riches.
A couch fit for the goddess is set in the center,
one made of polished Indian ivory draped with a purple
50   coverlet steeped in the crimson dye of the sea conch.
    Embroidered with various figures of men from past ages,
its marvelous art reveals the great prowess of heroes.
For there, staring out from the resonant seacoast of Dia,
Ariadne watches the swift fleet of Theseus leaving,
55   and in her heart an unrestrainable fury arises,
for she still can't believe that she sees what she is seeing!
—no wonder, for sleep had deceived her: just now awakened,
she finds herself coolly abandoned there on the seashore.

Ungrateful, her lover flees, striking the waves with his oarblades,
leaving the storm winds to make good on his broken promise.   60
The weeping daughter of Minos stands still in the seaweed,
stands watching him in the distance: a Maenad in marble,
rocked by the waves of her anguish, she stands there & watches;
her golden hair is no longer tied up in its headband,
the delicate veil no longer covers her torso,   65
her tender white breasts are no longer bound up in their halter;
all of her garments have slipped to her feet in confusion,
adrift in the salt tide that evenly scoured the coastline.
—Not that she noticed the headband or the veil floating
beside her, for it was you that she thought of, Theseus: 70
the wretched girl clung to you in complete desperation!
Venus of Eryx had driven her crazy with sorrow,
sowing the seeds of that thorny grief in her spirit
much earlier, back in that time when the adamant hero
set out from the curved shore of the port at Piraeus   75
and sailed to the Cretan quarters of the harsh King Minos.
    The story is that in those days the people of Athens
were forced by a plague to make restitution for slaying
one of the sons of King Minos by sending their finest
young men & maidens, a meal to the Minotaur's liking!   80
With these cares rocking the strait walls of his beloved city,
Theseus chose to offer himself as a victim,
rather than that any more of the living unliving
should be taken away from Athens to perish at Knossos.
So he set sail then, in a light boat, and favoring breezes   85
brought him to the tyrannous kingdom of greathearted Minos.
When she first caught sight of that handsome stranger, the royal
virgin (whose celibate couch still warmly enfolded
her in its maternal embraces, exuding the odors
of myrtle that grows on the banks of streams in Eurotas   90

and the varied flowers that whispering spring engenders)
Ariadne kept her eyes fixed on him until they took fire,
until that fire had traveled the length of her body
and made its way into even her innermost marrow!
95   O Cupid, you who arouse such extravagant passions,
forever mixing great joys & great sorrows together,
and you who rule upon Golgos & leafy Idalium,
what were the waves like, on which you tossed the poor maiden's
passionate heart as she sighed for her fair-haired stranger?
100   How many times in exhaustion did she know terror,
and find herself turning even paler than gold,
while he impatiently waited to take on that savage
in a fight which would end either with death or with glory?
The gifts of incense she'd offered while praying to heaven
105   in fearful silence were neither unwelcome nor wasted.
Think of an oak, or a conebearing pine tree that oozes
with rosin, shaking its branches high up on Mount Taurus;
one which a fierce storm, wrenching the grain of its timber
uproots & sends hurtling off to spread terrible havoc
110   for a great distance, until it lies prone in destruction:
then think of Theseus over the overcome monster
vainly tossing its horns in the unresisting breezes.
Unharmed—it had ended with glory—he felt his way back,
using a thin thread to guide his wandering footsteps,
115   or else, as he worked his way out of the labyrinth's windings,
its indiscernible maze would have left him bewildered.

   But why should I digress from my earliest subject,
and go on to tell how she turned from the face of her father
and the embrace of her sister, and lastly the mother
120   who grieved because she loved her daughter to distraction,
choosing the sweet love of Theseus over them all?
Or how she came to the foaming seacoast of Dia,

and how, when her eyes had been sealed up tightly in slumber,
her careless lover abandoned her & departed?
Often, they say, when her sorrow had turned into madness   125
that could not be silent, she uttered shrill cries of anguish,
and sadly worked her way up one of the steep mountains
to take a long look at the ocean's vast expanses:
then rushed abruptly down to plunge into the water,
lifting her clingy robe up over her bare leg;   130
and in her last moments of grief, in a voice broken
by sobs, she spoke, as chilly tears streamed down her face:
"So, you have torn me away from my family's altar
to leave me on this empty island, have you, Theseus?
—Gone off, ignoring the terrible justice of heaven,   135
sailing your god-damned cargo of lies back to Athens?
Could nothing, nothing at all, have turned that ferocious
mind of yours from this plan? Was there no tenderness lurking
within you, that might have urged you to offer me mercy?
For it wasn't *this* that you promised me ever so blandly,   140
it wasn't this at all that you led me to hope for
when you spoke of the happy marriage, the wedding we dreamt
       of—
words which the winds of heaven now tear into tatters!
Let no woman ever believe any oath that a man swears,
or ever expect him to keep faith with his fine speeches!   145
When they want something, when they are anxious to get it,
they take oaths without fear, and pour out their promises freely;
but just as soon as their hot desire is sated,
none of their lies & deceptions ever disturb them.
You know that when death whirled you around in confusion   150
I saved you, choosing to let my own brother perish,
rather than fail in my duty to you who've betrayed me!
And for my good service, I will be torn by birds & wild beasts

when my body lies here without any tomb to protect it.
155 What lion gave birth to you under a rock in the desert?
What sea conceived you, spewed you up out of its waters?
Or was it Syrtis, or Scylla, or dreadful Charybdis,
that you repay the sweet gift of life in this fashion?
If, in your heart, you never intended our marriage
160 for fear of what your stern father had earlier told you,
nevertheless you could have brought me into your palace
as a servant, whose pleasure it would have been to humbly
attend you, bathing your white feet in clear water
and laying the purple coverlet out in your chamber.
165 But why should I cry out in vain to the ignorant air,
a woman maddened by suffering? The air is senseless,
unable to hear me, unable to make any answer.
By now he must be nearly half-done with his journey,
and no one at all appears on this bare stretch of seaweed.
170 In my final moments, fortune cruelly mocks me,
denying me those who would listen to my lamentations.
O God almighty, I wish that they had never
landed at Crete, those ships that came sailing from Athens,
that the lying sailor had never come with his dreadful
175 payment for the wild bull, or moored his ships in our harbor,
wickedly hiding his bloodthirsty plot under a pleasant
façade, while he stayed as an honored guest in the palace!
Where can I go? What hope shall I cling to, abandoned?
Shall I seek the mountains of Sidon?—but a great gulf
180 of truculent water enforces my separation.
Or should I beg help from the father that I deserted
to follow a young man stained with the blood of my brother?
Console myself with the trustworthy love of a husband
who flees me, bending inflexible oars in the water?
185 Here there is nothing but shoreline, an unpeopled island

with no way of crossing over the sea that surrounds it,
no means of fleeing, no hope at all—everywhere silence,
emptiness everywhere—terrible death shows his face here.
Nevertheless, before I sink down into darkness,
and before all feeling fades from my weary body,   190
I will implore the gods for justice to right my betrayal,
and beg the protection of heaven in my final moments.
O Furies, charged with vengeance that punishes evil,
you whose bleak foreheads are girded with writhing serpents
which clearly display the outrage your cold hearts keep hidden,   195
come here to me quickly, listen to my lamentation,
which I deliver in pain from the depths of my passion,
unwillingly forced to, afire, blinded with madness!
—Since what I say is the truth, since I say it sincerely,
do not allow my lament to fade without issue: 200
but just as Theseus carelessly left me to die here,
may that same carelessness ruin him and his dearest!"
When she had emptied her heart of all of its sorrows,
anxiously seeking revenge for the way she'd been treated,
the ruler of heaven assented, majestically nodding,   205
and with that gesture the earth & the rough seas were shaken,
and the stars leapt in the firmament, quivering brightly.
But Theseus, in a dark mood which muddled his judgement,
let slip out of mind the instructions which he had clung to,
forgetting to raise the white sail which his father awaited,   210
the sweet sign that he was returning uninjured to Athens.
For they say that when Aegeus consigned his departing
son to the winds as his fleet left Athena's protection,
he first embraced the young man & then gave him these orders:
"My only son, dearer to me than even long life is,   215
whom I am forced to send off on a doubtful adventure,
although just restored to me at the end of my lifetime,

because my misfortune & your passionate courage
must take you away from me before my exhausted
220   eyes could have had their fill of your image before me,
I will not cheerfully let you leave here rejoicing,
or allow you to show any signs of fortune's good favor:
but first I will empty my heart of its wild lamentation,
soiling my white hairs with earth & a downpour of ashes,
225   and then hang dyed sails on your ship's swaying mastpole,
so that this grief of ours, this heart-wringing fire
will be proclaimed by sheets steeped in Iberian purple.
—Yet, if the goddess who dwells on sacred Itonus,
pledged to defend our people & the realm of Erectheus,
230   allows you to dabble your right hand in the bull's blood,
make certain that you remember these orders I give you
and keep them in mind no matter how long a time passes:
as soon as you catch your first glimpse of our hillside,
take every last vestige of mourning down from your yardarms
235   and set a white sail aloft in the twisted rigging,
so that the minute I see it, I'll understand—and gladly
welcome the fortunate hour of your reappearance!"
Theseus, at first, paid attention to these instructions,
but then they slipped from his mind, just as the wind-driven
240   clouds scatter from the snowy peak of a mountain.
His father, however, keeping vigil on the Acropolis,
wasting his eyes with tears that never stopped flowing,
when he first caught sight of those dark sails bellying outward
threw himself down from the rocky peak into the ocean,
245   believing that fate had cruelly taken Theseus.
So, when the hero entered his home, it was darkened
by mourning, and he received for himself as much sorrow
as he had thoughtlessly given the daughter of Minos,
who kept a sad watch as his ship sank into the distance,

dwelling on all of those cares with which she'd been wounded.   250
    But in another scene, flourishing Iacchus swaggered,
surrounded by drunken Sileni & wanton young Satyrs;
burning with love, he was searching for you, Ariadne.

. . . .

and Maenads also, who raged all around in a rapture,   255
crying "*Euhoe! Euhoe!*" as their heads crazily nodded.
Some of them whirled their weapons, spears tipped with vine-
        leaves;
some tossed about the limbs of a bull they'd dismembered,
and some were girding their bodies with writhing serpents
or worshipping ritual emblems kept hidden in baskets,   260
emblems which only initiates ever uncover.
Others with uplifted hands were beating their tambours
or shrilly clashing their hollow bronze cymbals together;
many of them had horns which were raucously blaring,
and the barbaric flute wailed out its hideous noises.   265
    Such were the figures which brightly adorned that rich hanging
whose ample folds lay over the couch of the goddess.
When the young Thessalians' desire to see it was sated
completely, they gave way to the gods descending from heaven;
you've seen the west wind rile the calm sea in the morning,   270
how it herds the steepening wavelets, sweeps them before it
as Dawn ascends to the gates of the journeying Sun;
those waves move slowly at first, urged on by a mild wind,
and advance with a muted sound of continuous laughter;
but after the wind has arisen, they run on together   275
and from a great distance they gleam with reflections of crimson:
so, moving out of the palace & out of its courtyard,
the mortal wedding guests drifted off in every direction.
After they left, the first to arrive from Mount Pelion's
summit was Chiron the Centaur, with pastoral presents;   280

for whatever grows wild in the fields or on the great mountains
of Thessaly, whatever the mild Favonian breezes
show in the way of flowers that grow beside rivers,
he brought along with him, all woven together unsorted,
285   and made the house laugh with odors that tickled the senses.
Directly came Peneus next, from evergreen Tempe,
Tempe, completely encircled by ominous forests,
leaving the nymphs of the vale to continue their dancing;
not empty-handed, he fetched along elegant beech trees
plucked up by their dangling roots, and the straight-stemmed
290   laurel
and nodding plane tree besides, and the pliant sister
of burnt-out Phaeton, as well as the towering cypress:
he wove these together in a continuous pattern
to make a green curtain of branches surrounding the courtyard.
295   After him followed Prometheus, known for invention,
still bearing the faded scars of that ancient atonement
which he had made while chained arm & leg to a mountain,
dizzily hanging from its precipitous summit.
Next came the father of gods with his immortal children,
300   all except you, alone up in heaven, Apollo,
you & your sister who dwells on the mountains of Idrus;
for she scorned Peleus too, even as you did,
and had no wish to honor the marriage of Thetis.

    After they'd settled themselves on the snowy white couches,
305   the tables before them were heaped with a various banquet.
Meanwhile, the Parcae began to chant their prophetic
song, swaying their bodies as they moved about infirmly.
Their ancient limbs were covered in gleaming white garments
which fell to their ankles; their robes were bordered in crimson,
and their snowy white heads were encircled by crimson
310   headbands:

their bony hands practiced the task they will practice forever.
The left hand held on to the distaff, wrapped up in soft wool,
and the right carefully drew the thread out, with the fingers
turned upward to shape it; then down went the thumb, and
      neatly
twirled the spindle poised on its circular flywheel;   315
and as they spun, they tugged the threads clean with their teeth:
bits of wool, which before had clung to the stuff they were
      working
now stuck to their poor withered lips in little dry tufts.
At their feet, baskets of plaited willow protected
soft bundles of gleaming fleece that lay ready for spinning.   320
And plucking the fibers, they chanted loudly & clearly,
uttered oracular speech in a sacred poem,
a poem no future age will condemn as untruthful:

"Heroic actions have made your name even more lustrous,
defender of Thessaly, dear to the ruler of heaven,   325
attend the true oracle which the three sisters deliver
on this festive day! As Destiny follows your motion,
run, spindles, run, drawing the threads that wait for the weaving.

Hesperus will be here soon with those gifts which the newly
married all long for; the bride will follow him closely,   330
flooding your heart with love that will charm you completely
as she lies by you at night in the tenderest slumber,
asleep with her delicate arms clasping your strong neck.
Run, spindles, run, drawing the threads that wait for the weaving.

No house before this has sheltered such a great passion,   335
no love has ever linked lovers in any such union
as this one which joins Peleus & Thetis together.
Run, spindles, run, drawing the threads that wait for the weaving.

Your son will be dreadful Achilles, unknown to Panic,
340   whose enemies never will see him retreating from battle;
often he'll easily win in long-distance races,
outstripping even the deer who advances like fire.
Run, spindles, run, drawing the threads that wait for the weaving.

No hero will dare to confront him in hand-to-hand combat
345   when the Phrygian fields are drenched with the blood of Trojans,
and Agamemnon, the third heir of deceitful Pelops,
tears down the walls of Troy when the long siege is over.
Run, spindles, run, drawing the threads that wait for the weaving.

Often the mothers of young sons about to be buried
350   will testify to his uncommon prowess in battle,
letting their unkempt hair fall loosely down to their shoulders
as they mar their withered breasts with their hands in
        bereavement.
Run, spindles, run, drawing the threads that wait for the weaving.

Just as a reaper hacks down the dense ears of ripe grain
355   under a burning sun, mowing the whole golden meadow,
Achilles will waste the young Trojans' limbs with his iron.
Run, spindles, run, drawing the threads that wait for the weaving.

The waves of Scamander will witness his heroic actions,
Scamander, which rushes into the stream of the Hellespont,
360   whose neck he will narrow by flinging up great piles of corpses
until its deep flood runs warm & red from the slaughter.
Run, spindles, run, drawing the threads that wait for the weaving.

But the last witness will be the gift given his spirit
in death, when the hero's high-heaped, circular mounded barrow
365   is graced with the snowy limbs of the sacrificed virgin.
Run, spindles, run, drawing the threads that wait for the weaving.

As soon as chance gives the exhausted Achaians the power
to keep the chains which Neptune wove from keeping his city,
that lofty tomb will be drenched with the blood of Polyxena,
struck down like a beast under the double-edged axeblade,   370
knees buckling as she pitches her headless corpse forward.
Run, spindles, run, drawing the threads that wait for the weaving.

Get going then, join those passions your hearts have desired;
now let the bridegroom take the goddess in fortunate union,
and let the bride be given right now to her eager new husband.   375
Run, spindles, run, drawing the threads that wait for the weaving.

The nurse who returns to attend her early tomorrow
will find that her neck can't be circled by yesterday's ribbon:
run, spindles, run, drawing the threads that wait for the weaving;

the worried mother who fears that her daughter is lying   380
alone will learn that her hopes for an heir aren't groundless!
Run, spindles, run, drawing the threads that wait for the weaving."

   So, in a prophetic spirit announcing the future
joy of Peleus, the Parcae once chanted their poem.
For the gods would frequent the worshipful homes of heroes   385
and show themselves present wherever men were assembled
before contempt had become the response to religion.
Often Jove the father, paying a regular visit
to one of his temples during the annual feast days,
would see a hundred bulls crash to earth in his honor.   390
And Liber would rove on the peak of Parnassus, driving
his Maenads, who shook their wild hair & cried out *"Euhoe!"*
Then all of Delphi came pouring out of the city
to greet the young god with smoke wreathing their altars.
And often in deathbearing warfare, Mars, or Athena   395
the mistress of Triton, or Nemesis, Virgin of Rhamnus,

would show themselves to encourage bands of armed men.
But after the earth had been imbued with hideous evil,
and men had abandoned all their desire for Justice,
400   when one brother had soaked his hands in the blood of another,
when children no longer wept at the deaths of their parents,
when a father could wish for the death of his very own son,
for the new stepmother seems to have found him attractive;
when an unwitting young man lay with his impious mother,
405   who had no fear of the shades of her deified parents,
then good & evil were confused in criminal madness,
turning the righteous minds of the gods from our behavior.
So they no longer appear now when mortals assemble,
and shun the light of luminous day altogether.

Though I'm exhausted by grief, by the unbroken sorrow
    that calls me away from the poetic virgins,
and too overwhelmed with my troubles to fetch you out any
    sweet signs of new life from the Muses, Ortalus—
for only a short while ago, the pale foot of my brother   5
    sank in the flowing waters of pitiless Lethe:
snatched from my sight, he lies restless under the alien
    soil of the Troad, below the beach at Rhoeteum.

. . . .

    never again will I set eyes on you, brother   10
more dear than life is: but surely I will always love you,
    always your death will have its place in my singing
as the nightingale sings under the dense-shadowed branches,
    mourning the fate of Itylus, gone from beside her. . . .
Nevertheless, in my sorrow, Ortalus, I send you   15
    a poem which I've translated from Callimachus,
so that you shouldn't imagine your words had been scattered
    to the aimless winds, put from my mind & forgotten,
just as the apple, a gift on the sly from her lover,
    falls from the perfectly blameless lap of the virgin: 20
oblivious wretch! She'd hidden it under her gown, but
    rises politely, seeing her mama—and sends it
hurtling out of its hiding place, bouncing & rolling
    while a self-conscious scarlet flows over her sad face!

He who observed every light in the vastness of heaven,
  who comprehended the stars' risings & settings
and how the bright swirling blaze of the sun comes to be
      darkened,
  how at fixed times the heavenly bodies grow dimmer,
5 how sweet Love summons Trivia from aerial orbit,
  concealing her in a cavern deep on Mount Latmus,
it was that man—Conon—who gazed up at heaven's threshold
  and saw *me* there, one of Berenice's flowing tresses,
shining in starlight—that same lock which she, in suppliant
      posture,
10   had temptingly offered to goddess after goddess
when the King (her husband for only a few brief hours)
  went off to wage a vengeful war on the Syrians,
and carried to battle the sweet traces of amorous combat,
  spoils which a virgin had yieldingly defended.
15 Is Venus *hated* by brides? Is that superabundance
  of tears which they shed outside the bridal chamber,
are they false tears—shed just to dampen the joys of their
      parents?
  Of course they are, really: I swear it by heaven!
My queen taught me this with all of her wild lamentation
20   when her new husband went off on his way to grim war.
What weeping there was then! But not—you say now—for a
      husband:
  it was a brother whose departure you lamented!
Well, whichever it was, I saw you devoured by sorrow,
  entirely preoccupied with your misfortune,
25 showing no sign of your spirit. But I who have known you

ever since childhood, I've never doubted your courage!
Or have you forgotten that boldness by which your royal husband
    was won, when no one else dared to be bolder?
But when that husband went off, what cries, what lamentation,
    both hands aglitter with your incessant bright tears!   30
What god so changed you? Or is it simply that lovers
    have little taste for any such long separations?
It was then that you poured out the blood of bulls, and offered
    me to the heavenly gods, for the safe homecoming
of your beloved. In no time at all he had added   35
    captive Asia to his own kingdom in Egypt.
And after that happened, I was received up in heaven,
    a novel payment for your old-fashioned prayer!
Unwillingly, O Queen, was I severed from your tresses,
    unwillingly! By you & by your head, I swear it!   40
And may anyone taking such oaths lightly be punished.
    But who can possibly stand up against iron?
Even the greatest of mountains which Helios glimpses
    when that bright son of Thia soars overhead, tumbled
when the Persians created a new sea & their young nobles   45
    sailed yachts right on through the middle of Mount Athos!
—now, when a *mountain* falls, what shall a mere lock of hair do?
    O God, may that whole race of Chalybes perish,
and the one who first went prying for underground iron
    and learned the skill of drawing it into firm bars!   50
My sisters & I had only a moment been parted:
    they were still in tears over me when the twin brother
of Ethiopian Memnon appeared—I mean Zephyr,
    the wingëd horse of Arsinoe the Locrian:
it was he who carried me through the cloud-darkened night, and   55
    gently deposited me on the chaste lap of Venus,
for the Grecian who lives on the shore of Canopus in Egypt

had sent her servant himself off on this errand.
And so that another gold crown might blaze on the spangled
60   threshold of heaven—besides the one that was taken
from Ariadne's head—Venus set us out to glimmer,
        devotees torn from the tawny locks of our mistress.
Borne to the place of the gods—but still bitterly weeping,
        I was fixed in place, a new star among the old ones.
65 You'll find me between the lights of the Virgin & Leo:
        I make my rounds next to Callisto, the daughter
of Lycaon, and spur on that dull laggard Boötes,
        who's always late at getting to bed in the ocean.
But though in the nighttime I move in heavenly circles,
70   daylight finds me resting with white-headed Tethys.
(Rhamnusian Virgin, allow me the license to speak up,
        for my truth will out—I won't be scared into silence,
not even if the stars cut me to pieces with sharp words:
        my loyal nature forces me into the open!)
75 This new condition displeases me more than it pleases,
        for I must be severed forever from my lady
right at that time when she's busy indulging her passion
        for those perfumes she was denied as a virgin!
Maids, when the torches you've longed for have seen you all
                married,
80   before you give yourselves to your husbands' desire,
before you undress & appear with your lovely breasts naked,
        remember to give me a pleasant sip from the onyx
jar which is yours who will keep yourselves decent in marriage.
        But, as for the one to whom foul adultery beckons,
85 may dust entirely blot her presumptuous libation,
        for I seek nothing from such as aren't worthy!
Rather, may Harmony dwell in your households forever,
        blissful young brides! And may Love also abide there;

and you, O Queen, when the brilliant lights are burning
and you stare up at the heavens, worshipping Venus,
remember your servant's current diminished condition
and of your largesse, make her a generous present.
Why must the stars detain me? I'd sooner be with my mistress,
and let Orion blaze beside Aquarius!

Greetings & salutations, Door—once dear to a cherished
   husband & to his father! God grant you good fortune!
They say that you used to work perfectly well for old Balbus
   back in the days when he himself was in charge here,
5   but now, since the old fellow died & his son has married,
   word is that you seem to have gone off your hinges.
Tell us what happened—why it is that you have changed so,
   why you're no longer as loyal to your new master.

DOOR:

I work for Caecilius now—may my words find his favor!
10   But *I'm* not to blame—even though everyone says so.
No one is able to pin any charges against me,
   yet Door must take the rap for what goes on inside,
and any time anything nasty turns up in the bedroom,
   everyone hollers at me, "It's all *your* fault, Door!"

CATULLUS:

15   A mere denial won't work very well to absolve you:
   let's have the story in all its sordid specifics!

DOOR:

Why should I bother? There's no one really anxious to hear it.

CATULLUS:

We'll listen—we'd love to! Come on, don't be so bashful.

DOOR:

Well, to begin with, the story she came here a virgin
20   just isn't true, although her first mate never touched her:
his little dirk dangled—a limp beet is scarcely more languid—
   and never managed to make a dent in his tunic.

But his father, they say, ravished her in his son's own bed,
  bringing disgrace down on that miserable household,
either because of an unsublimated libido   25
  or else just to give his impotent son a leg up,
since it required a rather more muscular item
  than his to ease her of her virginal constrictions.

CATULLUS:

How very obliging of this remarkable father
  to piss in his own son's lap! It's quite a story.   30

DOOR:

And it's quite well known, too—and not just locally either:
  Brixia, the town below the watchtower of Cycnus,
where the calm river Mella flows in a golden torrent,
  Brixia, mother of my beloved Verona,
tells of Postumius, mentions Cornelius also,   35
  with both of whom she's enjoyed illicit adventures!

CATULLUS:

At this point, someone might say, "Wait, Door—how can *you*
    know all that?
  You're not allowed to stray from your master's threshold,
or eavesdrop on people: fastened on vertical pivots,
  your only task is to open the house & close it."   40

DOOR:

Often I've overheard her, in furtive conversations
  discussing affairs alone with her servant women,
giving the names of the men I've just mentioned, as though she
  never imagined that I could hear her—or tattle.
Moreover, she spoke of another, whose name I *won't* mention,   45
  lest he show up here, twitching his fiery eyebrows:
a big man, who was once taken to court by some lying
  slut who insisted he'd started a baby in her!

POEMS • 99

"Fortune oppresses: affairs, miscarried, leave me bitter,"
    you say, and so you send me this tear-stained epistle,
pleading with me to *"raise up, restore from Death's very threshold*
    one of Life's castaways, shipwrecked, sea-tossed & stranded;
5   *one from whom Venus withholds post-libidinal slumbers,*
    a mateless man, forever estranged from his beloved,
unsolaced by those dulcet strains of the ancient poets
    when the anxious Soul tosses & turns in its vigil . . ."
I'm really pleased that you should remember our friendship,
10   and look to me for gifts of the Muses & Venus.
But I have my own griefs, Allius: and so that you shouldn't
    think I've grown bored with the obligations of friendship,
learn how the waves of misfortune have battered me also,
    and look for consolation from someone less wretched.
15   Since the day when I first put on the toga of manhood,
    in that unending springtime when nothing else mattered
but love & poetry, I've made both in abundance, far from
        unknown
    to that goddess whose cares all have a bittersweet flavor.
But all of my zeal for these passions died with my brother!
20   I mourn for you, my brother, so unkindly stolen,
for it is your death which has left me shattered completely:
    with you lie buried all of the hopes of our household,
with you have perished those pleasures which we held in
        common,
    pleasures nourished with your sweet love while you were
        living.
25   Because of your death I've put out of mind altogether
    the joyful discipline I once found so enthralling.

And so, when you write, *"it really is awkward, Catullus,*
    you being off at Verona, while her fine dandies
warm their chilly toes in the bed you've just gotten out of"—
    it's more than awkward, Allius: it's a disaster.   30
You'll understand then—my troubles keep me from giving,
    so if I don't offer, it's only because I'm unable.
In fact, though, I don't have many new poems with me,
    living as I do at Rome: that's where my house is,
the place in which I spend most of my time—just a single   35
    box of stuff—one out of many—follows me up here.
Since that's the case, please don't think that I'm simply too lazy
    to do it, or boorishly unsympathetic,
if I haven't offered you either of what you've requested:
    if I had them to send, I would have already sent them.   40

Muses, I can't remain silent concerning the matter
    in which I was so greatly aided by Allius,
or time as it rushes on through the oblivious ages
    will cover up that zeal of his in the night's blindness:
but I will tell you, that you may go on to tell many   45
    thousands, and see that these pages speak out forever

. . . .

    and after his death make certain his fame increases,
to keep the spider who spins in high places from weaving
    a shroud over the forgotten name of Allius.   50
For you know those griefs which I had been given by Venus,
    and how she slyly forced me right into the fire
when I was burning with as great a passion as Etna
    has, or the hot springs of Thermopylae in Malis;
and how my sorrowful eyes never rested from weeping,   55
    and my cheeks were never dry of that wretched torrent,
just as a glistening stream at the peak of a mountain

takes a quick leap from the edge of a mossy boulder
and plunges dizzily through a precipitous valley
60   until it crosses a roadbed crowded with people,
a joy to the traveller, ease from the sweat of his labors
    when summer's oppressive heat cracks open the parched fields!
or as a favoring breeze will spring up suddenly, aiding
    sailors near shipwreck in a raging storm's darkness,
65   saved by a vow which was sent up to Castor or Pollux:
    that was the kind of aid which my Allius offered.
He gave me access—a path to a field once forbidden,
    he gave me a house & gave me its mistress also,
and in that place we explored our mutual passion.
70   There my radiant goddess appeared to me, stepping
lightly & paused once—to stand with the sole of her sandal
    on the well-worn threshold as her bright foot crossed it,
as in that time when passionate love for her husband
    brought Laodamia to the house which Protesilaus
75   had built in vain, before the warm blood of sacrificial
    victims could calm the wrath of the rulers of heaven.
O Virgin of Rhamnus, never may anything please me
    which is begun without the consent of those rulers!
Laodamia learned, when Protesilaus departed,
80   how thirsty the altar is for the blood of victims,
forced to allow her new husband to leave her embraces
    before they had spent their second winter together,
whose long nights would have satisfied even her passion,
    and given her the strength to live on without him.
85   It happened quickly, the end which the Fates had predicted
    if he should go to the walls of Troy as a soldier.
For it was then that because of the capture of Helen
    Troy had invited the wrath of the Argive chieftains:

—damned Troy! The burial pit of both Europe & Asia,
   untimely grave of heroes & heroic actions!   90
Wasn't it Troy which brought sorrowful death to my brother?
   I mourn for you, my brother, so unkindly stolen,
and for the sweet light of life that is gone from your eyes now:
   with you lie buried all of the hopes of our household,
with you have perished those pleasures which we held in
      common,   95
   and which you nourished with your love while you were living!
Far away now from those burial places we visit,
   not resting among the ashes of your relations,
but in Troy—unspeakable, ill-omened Troy—you lie buried:
   at the world's end a foreign soil holds your body!   100
They say that the young men of Greece left their family altars
   then, and came rushing to Troy from every direction,
out to keep Paris from time spent with ravishing Helen
   at leisure, unchallenged in his peaceful chambers.
O lovely Laodamia, that event was the reason   105
   why a husband dearer than your life or spirit
was taken from you: the sea-surge of passion submerged you,
   sent you whirling over the edge of an abyss
as deep as those shafts which the Greeks say were sunk near
      Cyllene,
   to dry the rich soil once they had drained off the marshes: 110
Hercules drilled them, they say, through the side of the
      mountain,
   when his unswerving arrows transfixed the man-eating
birds of Stymphalia, slain while God's true son was serving
   a master who was unworthy of his servant,
to win immortality—and there, on heaven's threshold,   115
   to claim for his bride the virgin goddess Hebe.

But your love was even deeper than that deep abyss was,
    and taught you how to bear the yoke, untamed in spirit!
An old man cherishes his new grandson no more deeply,
120   watching him nurse in the arms of his only daughter:
born just in time to inherit the family fortune,
    his name is properly inscribed upon the tablets,
putting an end to the indecent glee of relations
    and driving the vulture away from the old man's head!
125 The snowy white dove never took such extravagant pleasure
    with her mate, although the dove is depicted
as endlessly feeding on kisses, outrageously wanton,
    much worse than *any* woman, no matter how ardent!
But you alone surpassed even these in their passion
130   when you & your golden husband lay together.
My darling lacked little or nothing of that perfection
    when she brought herself to lie in my embraces,
for Cupid was there and constantly flitted about her,
    the god resplendent in his bright saffron tunic!
135 So, if she must have others besides her Catullus, we'll suffer
    the infrequent lapses of our artful lady,
lest we should too much resemble respectable people:
    often even Juno, the greatest of goddesses,
gulps back her passionate rage at the sins of her husband,
140   knowing the countless tricks of promiscuous Jove!
But it's indecent, comparing men with immortals;

  . . . .

  . . . .

    you'll get no thanks for playing the bothersome parent.
145 Nor was she brought to me on the right hand of her father,
    out of a house made fragrant with Syrian incense,
but in the marvelous nighttime she came with those precious
    gifts she'd stolen right from the lap of her husband!

So it is really enough if she saves for us only
    those days she marks with the white stone of celebration . . .   150
For you, this gift of a poem—the best I could manage,
    Allius, in thanks for all of your many favors,
and in hopes that the passage of days one after another
    won't touch that name of yours with rust & corrode it.
And may there be added to this, those presents which Themis   155
    offered in ancient times to those who were worthy:
may you & your lady live in contentment together;
    joy to that house we played in, and to its mistress,
and to the one who first gave us . . .
    from whom all of our blessings had their beginning;   160
but far before all others, to one more dear than my soul is,
    my darling, whose life gives all my living its savor.

Rufus, stop asking why none of the young women ever
    wish to turn out a delicate thigh in your service,
not even when offered a bribe of almost transparent
    robes, or some cunning bit of expensive glitter.
Your chances are spoiled by a wicked rumor which claims you
    keep a foulsmelling goat penned up in your armpits!
The women all fear it. No wonder—it's really an awful
    beast which no pretty girl would have for a bedmate.
So either get rid of this wretched plague on our noses
    or else stop asking us why the women go running.

· 70 ·

My woman says there is no one whom she'd rather marry
   than me, not even Jupiter, if he came courting.
That's what she says—but what a woman says to a passionate
     lover
   ought to be scribbled on wind, on running water.

If anyone ever deserved such underarm goatodor
    or ever merited gout's terrible swellings,
it's that rival of yours, who's sharing not only your mistress
    but—quite miraculously—your diseases also!
Whenever he fucks her, both of them suffer your vengeance:
    she gets your goat & he's the one that your gout gets.

You used to say that you wished to know only Catullus,
    Lesbia, and wouldn't take even Jove before me!
I didn't regard you just as my mistress then: I cherished you
    as a father does his sons or his daughters' husbands.
Now that I know you, I burn for you even more fiercely,
    though I regard you as almost utterly worthless.
How can that be, you ask? It's because such cruelty forces
    lust to assume the shrunken place of affection.

· 73 ·

Give up expecting that anyone ever will thank you
   for anything, or show you gratitude ever.
All are ungrateful, and doing a kindness is nothing,
   or rather worse than nothing: a damaging nuisance!
So it is now with me—whom no one has hurt quite so badly
   as one who once called me his one and only true friend.

Gellius heard that his uncle was wont to rebuke any
    words or occasions even the *least* bit salacious.
So that he couldn't be chastised, he humped his own auntie,
    and her censorious husband found himself censored.
Gellius does as he pleases, now—for no matter how often
    uncle's fucked over, uncle won't utter a whisper.

To such a state have I been brought by your mischief, my Lesbia,
    and so completely ruined by my devotion,
that I couldn't think kindly of you if you did the best only,
    nor cease to love, even if you should do—everything.

If any pleasure can come to a man through recalling
   decent behavior in his relations with others,
not breaking his word, and never, in any agreement,
   deceiving men by abusing vows sworn to heaven,
then countless joys will await you in old age, Catullus,
   as a reward for this unrequited passion!
For all of those things which a man could possibly say or
   do have all been said & done by you already,
and none of them counted for anything, thanks to her vileness!
   Then why endure your self-torment any longer?
Why not abandon this wretched affair altogether,
   spare yourself pain the gods don't intend you to suffer!
It's hard to break off with someone you've loved such a long time:
   it's hard, but you have to do it, somehow or other.
Your only chance is to get out from under this sickness,
   no matter whether or not you think you're able.
O gods, if pity is yours, or if ever to any
   who lay near death you offered the gift of your mercy,
look on my suffering: if my life seems to you decent,
   then tear from within me this devouring cancer,
this heavy dullness wasting the joints of my body,
   completely driving every joy from my spirit!
Now I no longer ask that she love me as I love her,
   or—even less likely—that she give up the others:
all that I ask for is health, an end to this foul sickness!
   O gods, grant me this in exchange for my worship.

Rufus, whose friendship I vainly, unwisely believed in!
   —did I say *vainly?* Worse, for the cost was enormous!
Have you got into me, burning your way through my bowels,
   stealing from me all that I value in living?
Yes, you have stolen it all—you, the virulent poison
   of my life, the wretched plague of our friendship!

Gallus has two brothers: one married a beautiful woman,
   and the other has a son who's *very* attractive.
Gallus is darling: he coaxes this pair of young lovebirds
   until the pretty boy and pretty girl sleep together.
Gallus is senseless: he can't see his own marriage threatened
   by showing a nephew how to cuckold his uncle.

· · · · · · · · · · · · · · ·

  · · · · · · · · · · · · · ·

but now I *am* angry—because your scummy saliva
   has utterly fouled the chaste lips of a chaste girl.
You won't get away with it, really—Old Lady Rumor
   will tell all future ages what bad news you are!

Lesbius is pretty: boy, is he ever! Why Lesbia'd rather
   have him than you, Catullus, and your whole family!
Let prettyboy Lesbius sell us all—if he can find even three
   men of good taste to take his vile kiss when they meet him.

Gellius, what shall I tell them? They ask why your rosy
    lips are much whiter than even the snows of winter,
when you set out from home in the morning and when you
        awaken
    from your luxurious mid-afternoon siesta.
I don't know for certain, but isn't it true what they whisper:
    "The juicy fruit he favors / comes in human flavors . . ."
It must be: poor Victor's blue balls blurt out your vile secret
    just as your lips do, stained with his strained-off semen.

Was there no one, Juventius? No one? In all of the city,
    no darling man for you to go fall in love with,
besides this houseguest of yours from decaying Pisaurum,
    this stranger more jaundiced than a gilded statue?
Now you adore him and dare to thrust him before us,
    ignorant of what a criminal thing you are doing!

Quintius, if you wish Catullus to owe you his eyes or
    anything dearer to him than even his eyes are,
keep your hands off what is dearer to him than his eyes or
    dearer than anything dearer than his eyes are.

Lesbia hurls abuse at me in front of her husband:
   that fatuous person finds it highly amusing!
Nothing gets through to you, jackass—for silence would signal
   that she'd been cured of me, but her barking & bitching
show that not only haven't I not been forgotten,
   but that this burns her: and so she rants & rages.

Arrius had to have aitches to swell his orations,
    and threatened us all with *"hawful hinsidious hach-shuns!"*
He flattered himself on account of his great aspirations,
    for huffing as hard as he could, *"hit's hinsidious!"*
He got it, I guess, from his mother or his freeborn uncle
    or else from others of his mother's poor relations.
Our ears were relieved to learn that he'd been sent off to Syria:
    they still heard the same words, but without the hard
        breathing.
No longer fearful of hearing such speech in the future,
    we got, quite suddenly, a horrible message:
after the journey of Arrius, the huffed-at Ionian
    sea had acquired an aitch: now it's *Hionian!*

· 85 ·

I hate & love. And if you should ask how I can do both,
I couldn't say; but I feel it, and it shivers me.

Many find Quintia stunning. I find her attractive:
   tall, "regal," fair in complexion—these points are granted.
But stunning? No, I deny it: the woman is scarcely venerious,
   there's no spice at all in all the length of her body!
Now Lesbia is stunning, for Lesbia's beauty is total:
   and by that sum all other women are diminished.

No other woman can truthfully say she was cherished
  as much as Lesbia was when I was her lover.
Never, in any such bond, was fidelity greater
  than mine, in my love for you, ever discovered.

What *is* he up to, Gellius? What itch is he scratching
   in naked vigil there with his mother & sister?
What is the man up to, making his own uncle a cuckold?
   Have *you* any idea how great a sin he's committing?
—so great a sin that neither the waters of outermost Tethys
   nor Oceanus, father of Nymphs, could wash it away.
What worse could he stoop to, a man so thoroughly wicked?
   Suck his own cock? No, that would be an improvement.

Gellius is lean—but of course: with such an obliging mother
    (so hale & hearty!) such a venerious sister,
an uncle who's also obliging, and so many girlfriends
    (all kissing cousins!) how could he possibly fatten?
Why, even if he had relations *just* with relations,
    you'd find no end of reasons there for his leanness.

From those unholy deeds which Gellius does with his mother,
   let a Magus be born & brought up to tell fortunes,
for if we can trust the outrageous religion of Persia
   a Magus must come from an incestuous couple,
so he may honor the gods with sweet hymns to their liking,
   and render in flames the fatty bowels of slain beasts.

Really now, Gellius, I didn't think I could trust you
    in this unhappy affair, this wretched business
on the grounds that I knew you well, or thought you were loyal,
    or able to keep yourself from malicious mischief:
but because the woman I was so madly in love with
    wasn't your mother & wasn't a near relation,
and because I never imagined you would consider
    our mere friendship sufficient reason to shaft me.
You did, apparently—getting great pleasure from any
    business even the least bit tainted with viciousness!

Lesbia never avoids a good chance to abuse me
   in public, yet I'll be damned if she doesn't love me!
How can I tell? Because I'm exactly the same: I malign her
   always—yet I'll be damned if I don't really love her!

· 93 ·

I am not too terribly anxious to please you, Caesar,
nor even to learn the very first thing about you.

· 94 ·

Mentula fornicates. Fornicates? Mantool? Ah, surely
it's just as they say: *"The pot gathers its own potherbs."*

Nine years ago Cinna first began work on his poem
    and nine years later—at last—the *Zmyrna* is ready!
Meanwhile, Hortensius was churning out five hundred thousand
    . . . .

the *Zmyrna* is set on Cyprus, and Cyprus will read it;
    the very ages will age, perusing the *Zmyrna*,
while the *Annals* Volusius wrote will remainder in Italy,
    a cheap & all too abundant wrapping for mackerel.
My friend has written much in little—a virtue I cherish;
    but let the mob rejoice in that windbag Antimachus.

· 96 ·

If those in their silent graves can receive any pleasure
    or comfort at all, Calvus, from our lamenting,
from that desire with which we rekindle former affections
    and weep for friendships we long ago surrendered,
then surely her premature death brings less grief than
    joy to Quintilia, whom you continue to cherish.

Really, I shouldn't have thought that it made any difference
   whether Aemilius opened his mouth or his asshole:
one wouldn't expect to find elegance wafting from either.
   However, his asshole *does* show greater refinement,
since it has no teeth. The teeth in his mouth are enormous,
   set maladroitly in gums of saddlebag leather,
and when (as he's wont to) he grins, one thinks of the gaping
   cunt of a she-mule in heat, pissing profusely.
He fucks a great many women & thinks himself charming,
   but hasn't brains enough to walk a miller's donkey.
Surely the woman who went with him ought to take pleasure
   in licking clean a sickly old hangman's asshole.

What everyone says of pretentious, babbling asses
   fits you, if anyone, putrescent Victius:
that tongue of yours is perfectly suited for scouring
   the rudest rustic's leathery boots & asshole.
If you should ever decide to wipe us out utterly, Victius,
   open your mouth: just utter your wish & it's granted.

While you were teasing me, darling Juventius, I captured
    a tiny kiss, sweeter than the sweetest ambrosia.
I didn't get off with it, though—and haven't forgotten
    how you kept me on the rack for over an hour!
Profuse apologies followed, but all of my tears couldn't
    soften at all the sharpness of your cruel anger.
Soon as I did it, you fiercely commenced prophylaxis,
    washing your lips & rubbing them dry with your fingers
to cleanse the infection of *me* from your dear mouth completely,
    as though you'd been soulkissed by some virulent hooker!
Besides which, you handed me over to pitiless Cupid
    for ceaseless tortures in every conceivable fashion,
until my taste of ambrosial joy had been changed into
    a tiny kiss bitterer than the bitterest hellebore!
And so, since my wretched affection's so heavily punished,
    I promise that from now on I'll steal no more kisses.

Caelius wants Aufilenus: Quintius wants Aufilena:
   they die of passion for Verona's fairest flowers,
one for the brother, one for his sister. So that's what they mean by
   the saying about the "joys of brotherly friendship"!
Who am I backing? You, Caelius! For you once showed me
   unquestionable proof of your unique friendship
when a savage flame had seared through my bones to the
     marrow.
   So good luck, Caelius—and be a winner, lover!

Driven across many nations, across many oceans,
   I am here, my brother, for this final parting,
to offer at last those gifts which the dead are given
   and to speak in vain to your unspeaking ashes,
since bitter fortune forbids you to hear me or answer,
   O my wretched brother, so abruptly taken!
But now I must celebrate grief with funeral tributes
   offered the dead in the ancient way of the fathers;
accept these presents, wet with my brotherly tears, and
   now & forever, my brother, hail & farewell.

If there was ever one whom you could safely confide in,
 one whose fidelity wasn't a doubtful matter,
Cornelius, you will find that I'm sworn under sanction
 to be completely tightlipped, a model for Silence!

If you will kindly return my ten sesterces, Silo,
    then you can be just as boorish & bad as you want to.
But if you're pleased by the money I gave you, then keep it,
    pimp—and abandon your boorish bad behavior.

She is my life. Do you think that I could ever abuse her,
　　the woman dearer to me than my own eyes are?
I couldn't. But love her, if I weren't forced to? I wouldn't.
　　Ah, you & Tappo blow things out of proportion!

Mentula tried an assault on the mount of the chaste Muses:
scandalous scansions! They quickly forked him over.

· 106 ·

Seeing an auctioneer walking around with a lovely young boy,
what's one to think but, *Isn't he anxious for bidders?*

If ever something which someone with no expectation
  desired should happen, we are rightly delighted!
And so this news is delightful—it's dearer than gold is:
  you have returned to me, Lesbia, my desired!
Desired, yet never expected—but you *have* come back
  to me! A holiday, a day of celebration!
What living man is luckier than I am? Or able
  to say that anything could possibly be better?

If, by the will of the people, your old age, Cominius,
    fouled by indecent behavior, came to be ended,
I do not doubt that your tongue—such a good friend of evil!
    would be uprooted & fed to the greedy vulture,
nor that your gouged-out eyes would glide down the raven's black
        gullet
    while dogs took your bowels & wolves had the rest of you.

Darling, we'll both have equal shares in the sweet love you offer,
    and it will endure forever—you assure me.
O heaven, see to it that she can truly keep this promise,
    that it came from her heart & was sincerely given,
so that we may spend the rest of our days in this lifelong
    union, this undying compact of holy friendship.

A good whore, Aufilena, is always spoken of kindly:
   for when she's paid in advance, she's bound to deliver.
But you act unkindly—making, then breaking your promise,
   a great deal more eager to rake in than put out!
Either to do it—or else not to promise to do it,
   either'd be honest, Aufilena: but fraudulent
snatching reveals you as worse than the greediest hooker,
   who'll do it any way anyone wants her to do it.

Aufilena, to live in contentment with only one husband
   will bring the highest praise to a married woman.
But *really!* It's better to go down for almost anyone
   than be the mother of brothers by your own uncle!

You're just too much, Naso—too much for most men to handle,
    although you're certainly willing to handle most men.

Maecilia had—in Pompey's first consulship—only
  two lovers, Cinna; now that he's once again consul
the same two remain, though augmented: each by a thousand!
  Adultery's fecund seed thrives in a well-plowed soil.

His estate at Firmum is said to make Mentula wealthy,
   and so it should, with such an abundance of bounty,
all kinds of fowl, fish, pastureland, plowland, wild game for
       hunting—
   nevertheless, his expenses outpace its income.
So I don't mind hearing he's rich—as long as he isn't!
   I'm glad to praise this estate whose owner's a pauper.

Mentula has—all together—some thirty acres for grazing,
   forty for plowing: all the rest are liquid assets.
Surely the man must be wealthier than Croesus,
   having, in just one estate, such superabundance:
meadows & farmlands, great forests, deep marshes, extending
   all the way to the frozen North & the great Ocean!
Marvelous, all of this. Much more marvelous: Mentula's
   no man at all, but an overstuffed, outstanding mantool! Ah.

Often I scratched about, looking to see if I couldn't
    send you some of my translations of Callimachus,
hoping that they would soften you toward me, keep you from
       trying
    to shoot your venomous arrows right at my head.
Now I can see that the troubles I went to were wasted,
    Gellius, for all my prayers have gone unanswered.
So I must roll up my cloak as a shield from your missiles:
    but when you're shafted, you'll soon be begging for mercy.

A CHRONOLOGY

NOTES ON THE POEMS

In 84 B.C. Gaius Valerius Catullus was born at Verona, which was then the principal city of the Roman province of Cisalpine Gaul, located on the Italian side of the Alps, north of the river Po. Inhabitants of the province were called Transpadanes. Catullus came from a wealthy family: in addition to a home in Verona, he mentions an apartment in Rome, a suburban hideaway outside the city, and a villa at Sirmio. His father was a friend of Julius Caesar, who maintained their friendship even after Catullus wrote the poems about Mamurra, which, Caesar admitted, had greatly damaged his own reputation.

The poet had a brother to whom he was deeply attached and by whom he was encouraged to write poetry. Catullus began writing at an early age, influenced by the work of the neoterics, a group of poets then beginning to get attention in Rome. Inspired by the earlier Greek poets of Alexandria, especially Callimachus, the neoterics produced poetry that was highly self-conscious, technically sophisticated, and radically innovative. Among this group were Catullus's close friend and collaborator, Gaius Licinius Calvus Macer, his fellow Transpadane (and perhaps his teacher), Valerius Cato, and Gaius Helvius Cinna.

At what point he began his relationship with the woman he called Lesbia, we do not know, nor can we say with certainty that we know who Lesbia was. Over the years, however, a very good circumstantial case has been made for Clodia Metelli, sister of the notorious demagogue, Publius Clodius Pulcher, and wife of Quintus Metellus Celer, who was posted to Cisalpine Gaul as governor in 62. When Metellus died in 59, Clodia began an affair with Cicero's young protégé, Marcus Caelius Rufus. If Rufus was in fact

Catullus' rival for Clodia, then poems 58, 69, and 77 become a great deal clearer.

Around the year 58, Catullus' brother died and was buried in Asia Minor. In poem 68, written shortly after the brother's death, he makes it clear that his relationship with Lesbia was another source of grief. From 57 to 56, Catullus served in the province of Bithynia with his friend, the poet Gaius Cinna, as part of the entourage of Gaius Memmius, who had been posted to the province as governor. At that time, he apparently visited the grave of his brother.

On his return to Italy, he seems to have gone first to Sirmio and then to Rome, where poem 11, among others, suggests that Lesbia attempted a reconciliation, which he spurned. It was probably at this time that Catullus repaired his relationship with Julius Caesar, apologizing to him for the poems he had written earlier about Mamurra. Caesar, says the historian Suetonius, responded to the poet's apology by inviting him to dinner that same day.

In 54 B.C. Catullus died at Rome.

Although Catullus is almost indecently accessible to modern readers, there are poems of his which either demand or request some explication. In these notes I have tried to explain the situation of the poet in relation to his immediate audience, where that situation would not be obvious to modern readers. I have also attempted to provide incidental information about aspects of Roman life with which modern readers may be unfamiliar and to identify the places and the people in the poems. These notes are meant to forestall elementary misunderstandings between the poet and his readers; they are not intended to take the place of the detailed scholarly commentaries on the poems of Catullus included in the editions of E. T. Merrill (Cambridge: Harvard University Press, 1951), C. J. Fordyce (Oxford: Oxford University Press, 1961), and Kenneth Quinn (New York: Macmillan & Company, 1970). Anyone familiar with their work will realize the extent of my indebtedness to it, here gratefully acknowledged; it could not have gone without saying that whatever errors of fact or judgement may be found herein are my own. Readers may also wish to seek out A. L. Wheeler's *Catullus and the Traditions of Ancient Poetry* (Berkeley: University of California Press, 1934), E. A. Havelock's *The Lyric Genius of Catullus* (Oxford: Oxford University Press, 1939), Kenneth Quinn's *The Catullan Revolution* (Ann Arbor: University of Michigan Press, 1969), and Charles Martin's *Catullus* (Hermes Books, New Haven: Yale University Press, forthcoming).

1

This poem dedicates a small collection of the poet's work to *Cornelius Nepos*, biographer, historian, and fellow Transpadane. The universal history to which C. here refers, the *Chronica*, did not survive.

1B

Two fragments that once, perhaps, made a single poem, sundered by an accident of transmission; the first three lines occur after poem 14 and the last three after poem 2. Warned against marriage by an oracle, the virgin *Atalanta* challenged each of her suitors to a footrace and then speared him in the back when she caught up. Hippomenes avoided this fate by dropping three golden apples, a gift from Aphrodite, in her path. Atalanta stopped for the irresistible trinkets and lost the race. (The oracle proved accurate: see note on poem 63, l. 76.)

2

Attempts have been made to replace the all-too-common *sparrow* with a more elegant or attractive pet; the blue rock thrush and the chaffinch have both had their partisans, but a team of domestic sparrows draws the chariot of Aphrodite in one of Sappho's poems, a detail which surely would have appealed to C. The mistress is generally, though not universally, taken to be Lesbia.

3

Venuses and Cupids: C. uses the plural to show the intensity of his feelings. *Orcus* is the Roman god of the dead, whose name came to be symbolic of the underworld.

4

C. celebrates the illustrious career and impending retirement of the yacht which carried him safely back from Bithynia to the tranquil waters of Lake Benacus at Sirmio (now the Lago di Garda at Sirmione), where the poet's father had a villa. The earlier part of that journey is rehearsed in lines 6–11. *Amastris, Cytorus:* ports on the Black Sea. C. is to be imagined as addressing his guests at Sirmio, in the presence of either the yacht or a small votive model, which he is offering up to Castor and Pollux, twin sons of Leda and Zeus, the protectors of seafarers.

5

Lesbia is a pseudonym concealing the identity of a woman who is gener-
ally, though not universally, taken to be the notorious Clodia Metelli, sis-
ter of the populist demagogue Publius Clodius Pulcher. To C.'s audience,
the pseudonym would have immediately and strikingly conjured up the
refined sensuality of Sappho of Lesbos.

6

Flavius is otherwise unknown.

7

A whimsically erudite development of the theme of poem 5. *Cyrene* was a
Libyan city, famous as a source of the medicinal herb laserpicium or *sil-
phium*, known to our grandparents as asafoetida. The *shrine of Jupiter* was
actually a temple of Ammon, the corresponding Egyptian deity. *Battus*
was the legendary founding father and first king of Cyrene. Callimachus,
the third century Greek poet whom C. admired and translated, was born
in Cyrene and called himself Battiades, son of Battus.

9

Veranius is otherwise unknown, though apparently a close friend not only
of C. but of C.'s friend Fabullus, with whose name his is linked in poems
12 and 47.

10

Written after C.'s return from Bithynia in 56 B.C. The identity of *Varus* is
uncertain and unimportant. *Serapis* was an Egyptian deity, imported to
Rome in the second century; there might be a hidden subtext in the
woman's devotion to this particular goddess. *Gaius Cinna*, who accom-
panied C. on his journey to Bithynia, was a neoteric poet, whose desper-
ate attempt to unconfuse the mob ("I am Cinna the poet . . . I am not
Cinna the conspirator!") did not save him from dismemberment ("Tear
him for his bad verses!") after the death of Shakespeare's Julius Caesar.
Cinna's long poem, the *Zmyrna*, is praised by C. in poem 95.

11

Furius and *Aurelius* have sworn to accompany C. anywhere in the Roman
world he might wish to go; in return, he offers them a mission more chal-

lenging than travel abroad could offer. The *Hyrcani* lived on the southern shore of the Caspian Sea; along with the Arabians they were enemies of Rome, as were the *Parthians*, fierce cavalrymen, distinguished for their archery. Julius *Caesar* crossed the *Rhine* in the summer of 55 B.C. and invaded Britain in the fall. The *Sagae* (Scythians) were nomads living in Persia.

12

Romans brought their own napkins with them when they dined out; napkin-snatching seems to have been a not-uncommon nuisance. *Asinius* is Marrucinus Asinius; his brother, Gaius Asinius *Pollio*, was a distinguished orator and historian. *Veraniolus* is an affectionate diminutive of Veranius.

13

Fabullus: an important friend of C.; sometimes paired with Veranius and, like him, otherwise unknown.

14

Calvus is Gaius Licinius Calvus Macer, an important neoteric poet, an orator of distinction, and a close friend of C. On several occasions he successfully prosecuted Publius *Vatinius. Sulla* is otherwise unknown, though schoolmasters were proverbially impecunious. The *Saturnalia* was a Roman festival held between 17 and 23 December to honor the Italian god Saturnus. It was a time of banqueting, merrymaking, and giftgiving. *Suffenus* (discussed in some detail in poem 22), *Caesius*, and *Aquinus* are otherwise unknown, but presumably represent man's ability to produce bad poetry in variety and abundance.

15

Is the young beloved Juventius? Is the poet serious? The punishment for adultery given in the last lines of this poem was traditional, but one suspects that it was honored more in the breech than in the observance.

16

C.'s threat would have struck his Roman audience as an altogether appropriate response to a dastardly provocation: extremism in the defense of one's virility was no vice.

17

The *rites of Salisubsalis* were evidently very energetic performances in honor of some deity, whose identity is no longer known. *Liguria:* an area on the northwestern coast of Italy. *Iron-shod footgear:* Roman horses and donkeys wore leather socks with metal soles that were tied onto their legs, an insecure arrangement when roads turned muddy.

22

A *Suffenus* is mentioned in poem 14, a *Varus* and his new mistress in poem 10. The *good new rolls* are indicative of a deluxe edition. The papyrus was lined with a circular lead plate, and the rough edges were smoothed with pumice. The volume was rolled on an ivory shaft with protruding knobs at either end and encased in a protective wrapper of parchment.

24

The *flower / of all Juventians* cannot be identified. C.'s repetition of the first line from poem 23 indicates that his rival for the boy's affections was Furius. *Midas:* fabled Phrygian king, whose touch turned everything to gold.

25

Thallus is otherwise unknown.

26

In the original, C. puns on the word *opposita*, which means both "facing" and "mortgaged."

27

Falernian: one of the most popular of Italian wines. *Postumia:* At parties, a Master of Revels was chosen by a throw of the dice; it was his role to preside over the making of toasts and to dictate the strength of the drinks (Romans customarily diluted their wine with more than an equal amount of water). Both the undiluted wine and the presence of a Mistress of Revels would have been unusual, if not somewhat scandalous. *Bacchus*, the god of wine, here lends it his name.

C. greets his friends Veranius and Fabullus, who have been serving with L. Calpurnius *Piso* in Macedonia, and reminisces about his unprofitable labors in Bithynia under Gaius *Memmius*. *Romulus* and *Remus* were the legendary founders of Rome.

A poem against Julius *Caesar* and his new son-in-law, *Pompey* (Gnaeus Pompeius Magnus), in the form of an attack on the conspicuous consumption of their mutual protégé, *Mamurra*. Mamurra inspired more poems of invective than any of C.'s other enemies: was it just his lavishness, or was he perhaps a rival of the poet? This poem was probably written between Caesar's first invasion of Britain in 55 B.C., which inspired extravagant hopes of the wealth to be found there, and his second invasion in 54 B.C., which shattered them. *Romulus:* Julius Caesar, seen as the decadent heir to the legendary founder. *Adonis:* the lover of Aphrodite, whose pet was the *dove cock. Pontus:* Caesar served in the army of the governor of Pontus in 79 B.C. Caesar's *Spanish adventure* was a very profitable expedition to Lusitania in 61 B.C.

The identity of *Alfenus* is unknown. *Good Faith:* the Roman god *Fides* held men accountable for their promises.

C. expresses his delight at returning safely to *Sirmio* from the province of Bithynia. *Lydian waters:* the area had originally been settled by Etruscans, who were thought to have come there from Lydia.

The classic note on this poem is E. T. Merrill's: "Contents execrable. Date, indeterminable. Metre, Phalaecean." (Merrill, p. 59) *Ipsitilla* is otherwise unknown.

Vibennius and his son are otherwise unknown.

34

A hymn to the goddess *Diana*, describing her ancestry and attributes, to be sung by a chorus of boys and girls at a feast in her honor. *Latona's child:* Leto (Roman Latona) was the mother of twins, Artemis (Diana) and Apollo. Zeus was their father. *Delos:* smallest of the Cycladic Islands and Diana's legendary birthplace. *Juno, Trivia,* and *Luna* were three different ways of naming and invoking the goddess: Juno assisted women in labor; Trivia (or *Hecate*) was goddess of the underworld, worshipped at crossroads; Luna was the goddess of the moon.

35

Caecilius of Comum (now Como) is otherwise unknown. His poem has not survived, but its title indicates that the poem dealt with the goddess Cybele. *Dindymus* was a mountain sacred to her worship in Phrygia. (See note on poem 63.) The *Sapphic Muse:* Sappho. C.'s compliment suggests that his friend's admirer might have been a poet herself.

36

Lesbia, or another friend, has perhaps said something like, "He's the worst of poets—before I get back together with him, I'll see his books burnt like trash!" C. pretends to misunderstand. *Volusius* and his *Annals,* further disparaged in poem 95, are otherwise unknown. *Gimpy Vulcan:* husband of Venus, the god of ironworking, crippled by the Olympians to prevent him from running off with the secrets of his trade; the metrical feet of Volusius are similarly clumsy. *Idalium, Urii,* etc.: towns noted for the worship of Venus.

37

Egnatius is known only from this poem and poem 39.

38

Cornificius is possibly Quintus Cornificius, orator, man of letters, and officer of Julius Caesar. *Simonides* of Ceos was famous for his lyric dirges. *Hercules:* the legendary hero of the twelve labors, who became a god after his death.

40

Poor little *Ravidus* is otherwise unknown.

44

A small joke at the expense of one Publius *Sestius*, friend and associate of Cicero. He writes in a style that the Romans described as *frigidus*, and C. pretends that the mere reading of one of his speeches has given him a chill. "*Sabine* . . . or . . . *Tiburtine*": the former address had rustic associations, the latter, cachet.

45

Septimius and *Acme* are otherwise unknown. It is difficult to believe that this poem is as uncomplicatedly idyllic as it appears to be. The *great heap of Syrias and Britains* represented the eastern and western ends of Roman imperial ambitions at that time: in 55 B.C., Crassus led an expedition into Parthia, and Caesar invaded Britain.

46

A poem anticipating the poet's departure from Bithynia and a sightseeing tour of Greece before returning home to Italy. *Zephyr:* the west wind. The *plains of Troy* were located in the province of Bithynia. *Nicaea* was an important city in the province.

49

Marcus Tully is Cicero: the reason for C.'s gratitude, if it is genuine and not ironic, is unknown.

50

The poet addressed is C.'s very close friend, Gaius *Licinius* Calvus Macer. *Nemesis* was the Greek goddess of retribution, who punished murderers and perjurers.

51

The first three stanzas are an imitation of one of Sappho's extant odes; the last stanza is not. Poem 51 is one of only two of C.'s poems—the other is poem 11—in the Sapphic meter. It is often taken to be the first that he wrote to Sappho, and poem 11 is often taken as the last.

52

Nonius is unknown. *Vatinius:* the enemy of C.'s friend Calvus.

54

Apparently an attack on Julius Caesar, though no one has succeeded in making sense of what E. T. Merrill described as an "incurably defective" text (Merrill, p. 88). The names are unidentifiable.

55 & 58B

Camerius, otherwise unknown, is hiding out: C. has been looking for him everywhere, from the Circus Maximus to the temple of Capitoline Jove. *Pompey's portico* was part of the theater he built in the Campus Martius. Here Catullus invokes a collection of classical superheroes, distinguished for their velocity. *The Cretan Giant,* a bronze watchman commissioned by the legendary King Minos, ran around Crete three times a day in order to prevent invasion. *Pegasus:* the winged horse identified with a certain magazine of verse. *Perseus:* the hero who slew Medusa and rescued Andromeda. *Ladas:* a legendary Spartan runner. *The white horses of the Thracian King* were, needless to say, famous for their speed.

56

The important neoteric poet and critic Valerius *Cato* might have found this anecdote amusing.

58

Caelius is probably Marcus Caelius Rufus, protégé of Cicero and lover of Clodia Metelli. *Remus* is one of the legendary founders of Rome; the reference is ironic.

59

Rufa, Menenius, and *Rufulus* are all otherwise unknown, though Rufulus, a contemptuous diminutive of Rufus, might be Marcus Caelius Rufus. Funeral offerings of food were burned along with the bodies of the dead.

60

No one before G. P. Gould seems to have noticed that, in the original, the first and last letters of each line spell out a secret, complementary message: *natu ceu aes:* from birth, like bronze. The identity of the addressee is unknown. *Scylla:* a rock in the strait of Messina, opposite the whirlpool of Charybdis, between Italy and Sicily.

A poem celebrating the marriage of one Manlius Torquatus to a woman whom C. refers to as Junia (or Vinia) and Aurunculeia: nothing more is known about her. The groom was quite possibly the Torquatus known to his contemporaries as an exponent of Epicureanism and a supporter of Pompey, with whose forces he died fighting in Africa in 47 B.C.

The marriage poem was a common genre in C.'s time, and his version of it here is, in the words of C. J. Fordyce, "a fantasy in which the traditional topics of the genre and Hellenistic formulae are combined with a vivid and colourful representation of some of the main features of a Roman wedding" (Fordyce, p. 235).

C. functions in the poem as a very busy master of ceremonies. First he invokes Hymenaeus, the Greek god of marriage, and elaborates upon the deity's importance to human life and to the occasion at hand. Next he announces the appearance of the bride, who is somewhat hesitantly preparing to begin the journey from the house of her father to that of her husband. C. encourages her progress by making much of her looks and of the happiness in store for her husband; he then changes the tone of the poem sharply with the so-called Fescennine verses, which poke mildly bawdy fun, mainly at the groom, in order to prevent the gods from becoming jealous of the couple's bliss. C. escorts bride and bridal party into the bridal chamber where the groom is discovered, already in place on the couch that the couple will share. C. offers a prayer for their fruitfulness and then departs with the rest of the company, after urging the couple to get on with the pleasurable business at hand.

1	*You:* The god Hymenaeus was the son of *Urania*, the Muse of astronomy. *Mount Helicon* was the home of the Muses.
4–5	*O Hymenaee . . . .:* a ritual cry.
6–10	Hymenaeus is dressed in the traditional costume worn by a Roman bride.
18–19	*Paris* awarded Aphrodite (Roman *Venus*) the prize for beauty over Hera and Athena when the three goddesses were competing for the gift of a golden apple.
30	*Aganippe:* the nymph as personification of the spring sacred to the Muses where they dwell on Mount Helicon.
126–27	*Fescennine verses:* Romans derived the term from a town called Fescennium, but it probably came from *fascinum*, the evil eye.
135	*Talasio:* the Roman version of Hymenaeus.

Another marriage poem. This one cheerfully mixes Greek and Roman wedding motifs. It begins at the end of a Greek wedding feast, which preceded the actual ceremony itself. As was customary, men and women are seated on opposite sides of the room. The men first notice that the evening star has risen: at this point in a Roman wedding, the bride would set out from her father's house to that of her husband, and so the men rise up in eagerness. (At a Greek wedding, the bride would already have been present.) The women, apparently unable to see the star from where they are sitting, notice the actions of the men and get up to face them. Suddenly confronted, the men realize how ill-prepared they are for what will follow, and desperately try to get their act together before the singing contest begins with the second chorus of the young women.

1	*Vesper:* the evening star, which, like the morning star, is actually the planet Venus.
5	*Hymen . . . :* The ritual cry seems to have no other purpose than to signal the end of a passage.
7	*Oetean fire:* There was apparently a religious cult on Mount Oeta that celebrated the rising of the evening star.
20	*Hesperus:* another name for the evening star.
35	*Eous:* the morning star.

63

The story of a young man named Attis, who castrates himself in an irreversible act of consecration to the goddess Cybele, and then awakens to realize the true nature of his loss to lament what he has made of himself. The action of the poem takes place in Phrygia, site of Troy and legendary home of the goddess, and at that time a part of the province of Bithynia, which C. visited in 57–56 B.C.

According to somewhat dubious Roman legend, the cult of the goddess Cybele was imported to Rome from Phrygia in 204 B.C., after the Sybilline oracle revealed that Rome would be victorious over Carthage if she sheltered Cybele, who was then brought to the city and eventually housed in a temple on the Palatine, where she was served by her castrated priests, known as Gallae.

Romans were of two minds about her from the first: The aristocrats, fond of tracing their lineage back to the fall of Troy, were particularly devoted to her cult. Nevertheless, for these same Roman patriarchs, deliberately undramatic in their ordinary habits of worship, obsessed by their own virility, and suspicious of all things Eastern, the sight of a troupe of ullulating eunuchs, accompanying themselves on flutes, cymbals, and tambours while carrying a statue of the goddess through the streets of Rome, must have seemed a spectacle of abominable fascination. In C.'s time, Roman citizens were prohibited from taking part in her worship.

The legend of Attis and Cybele offered C. the opportunity to write a poem in which he could give dramatic scope to themes of importance in his culture, and, at the same time, create an allegorical representation of his own relationship with Lesbia. On one level, poem 63 is a dramatization of public attitudes of attraction and repulsion toward this powerful and frightening goddess, the mother who gives life but demands total subservience in return. On another, more personal level, C. can explore the psychological state of a young man unstrung by his passion and enthralled by an overwhelmingly powerful mistress, who has robbed him and countless others of their manhood. This, of course, is the theme of many of the poems to and about Lesbia.

3   *Attis:* The stories about him were numerous and often contradictory. He is usually a handsome young shepherd of (sometimes) divine origin with whom Cybele falls in love; he castrates himself out of his devotion to her.

23   *Maenads:* Maenads were, strictly speaking, the devotees of Dionysus, but the orgiastic activities of his devotees were much like those of Cybele's.

30   *Mount Ida:* a mountain in Phrygia associated with the cult of the goddess.

42–43   *Pasithea:* one of the Graces, promised in marriage to *Somnus*, god of sleep.

76   *her chariot's lions:* Cybele was accompanied by a pair of lionesses. According to one legend, Hippomenes forgot to thank Aphrodite for the gift of the golden apples that won him Atalanta, and the goddess, miffed, turned the newly wed pair into Cybele's leonine consorts.

91   *Mistress of Dindymus:* Dindymus was another Phrygian mountain associated with the worship of Cybele, who was often invoked as "Mistress of Mountains."

64

Our only surviving example of the long poem as practiced by the neoterics, poem 64 demonstrates the erudition and concern for craftsmanship that came into Roman poetry with their work. It is also warmly sensual, vivid in its description, and emotionally powerful.

It is customarily described as a narrative poem about the marriage of Peleus and Thetis, but the reader who comes to it looking for the elements of epic on the one hand or the elements of modern fiction on the other is going to be disappointed. It is hardly a narrative at all, in the conventional sense. Rather, the poem is a complex and subtle exploration of the relationship between the divine order and the human, a meditation on the themes of marriage and fidelity, seduction and betrayal, illustrated by the best examples that classical mythology and art had to offer.

The key to the poem is in its structure, and the complexity of that structure reminds us that the term "Alexandrian" once meant elegance as well as erudition. Poem 64 is composed of eight distinct tableaus, each made up of one or more related scenes, as follows:

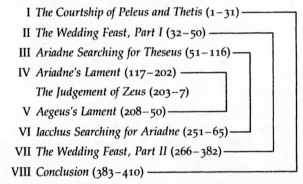

I *The Courtship of Peleus and Thetis* (1–31)

II *The Wedding Feast, Part I* (32–50)

III *Ariadne Searching for Theseus* (51–116)

IV *Ariadne's Lament* (117–202)

   The Judgement of Zeus (203–7)

V *Aegeus's Lament* (208–50)

VI *Iacchus Searching for Ariadne* (251–65)

VII *The Wedding Feast, Part II* (266–382)

VIII *Conclusion* (383–410)

The tableaus vary considerably in size, though they are responsive to a very basic kind of symmetry: the first four tableaus occupy 202 lines and the last four occupy 203 lines; they are joined together by a hinge, consisting of a single sentence of five lines. These tableaus form a "ring" structure: that is to say, the first and eighth tableaus deal with the contrast between the ways in which mortals and immortals mingled in the heroic age and in the present; the second and seventh tableaus describe the wedding feast. The four inner tableaus are descriptions of scenes embroidered on a coverlet in the bridal chamber: in the third and sixth tableaus two lovers search for their absent beloveds; in the fourth and fifth tableaus, Theseus brings grief to two different characters in two different ways. In the hinge at the exact center of the poem, Jupiter passes divine judgement on his perfidy. Such an outline illustrates, but does not exhaust, either the elegance of the concept or the possibilities for secondary relationships between tableaus.

Notes to individual references within this poem will be given under the heading of each tableau.

I. *The Courtship of Peleus and Thetis* (1–31): the hero Peleus and the sea nýmph Thetis meet when he, aboard the *Argo*, a ship built from the timbers of Mount Pelion with the divine aid of Athena, has set out from Greece with the other Argonauts, to capture the Golden Fleece from King Aeetes of Colchis.

17 *Nereids:* legendary sea nymphs, the daughters of Nereus and Doris.

21 *the Father:* Zeus, who had planned on marrying Thetis himself but was warned by an oracle that her son would be greater than his father.

30 *Tethys:* Tethys married her brother Oceanus and gave birth to Nereus, who married *his* sister, Doris, who gave birth to Thetis and the other Nereids.

31 *Ocean:* Oceanus, originally conceived of as the riverrun that wraps the world, was later personified.

II. *The Wedding Feast, Part I* (32–50) consists of two very brief scenes: in the first, the mortal wedding guests gather in Pharsalus (32–43); in the second, we are given a view of the interior of the palace (44–50).

36–38 A list of Thessalian cities: *Cieros* (or Cierium) is a town mentioned by Strabo. *Tempe* is the valley through which the river Peneus flows in the north of Thessaly; C. calls it *Phthiotic* after Phthiotis, far to the south. *Crannon* and *Larissa* were important towns in central Thessaly. Pharsalus: the seat of Peleus.

III. *Ariadne Searching for Theseus* (51–116): the first of four tableaus set on the coverlet in the bridal chamber. This tableau consists of two scenes: the first is of the awakened Ariadne, staring out at the blank ocean, searching for Theseus, who has left her sleeping on the island of Dia as he makes his way back to Athens. The second scene consists of a digressive cutback to the source of her sorrows: the arrival of Theseus at Crete, her falling in love with him, his slaying of the Minotaur with her help, and their departure together.

61 *Minos:* King of Crete.

62 *a Maenad:* The Maenads were female followers of Dionysus, who rescues and marries Ariadne; she is thus a Maenad by anticipation, though C. may simply be referring to her frenzied state at this point.

72 *Venus of Eryx:* Mount Eryx, in western Sicily, site of a famous temple of the goddess.

75 *Piraeus:* the seaport of Athens.

80 *the Minotaur:* Pasiphae, wife of Minos, fell in love with a bull by whom (with a little help from Daedalus) she conceived the Minotaur. Minos concealed his difficult stepson in the laby-

rinth at *Knossos*, where it battened on human sacrifices until Theseus, guided by a thread given him by Ariadne (the Minotaur's half sister) found his way into the monster's presence and dispatched him.

97   *Golgos and leafy Idalium:* on Cyprus, where Venus was held in particular esteem.

107   *Mount Taurus:* a mountain in southern Asia Minor, most likely chosen for its name.

IV. *Ariadne's Lament* (117–202): after a brief recapitulation of the events that brought her here, Ariadne goes into the lengthy monologue in which she pours out her sorrow and rage.

157   *Syrtis:* shallows off the coast of Africa. *Scylla:* the rock in the strait of Messina, opposite *Charybdis,* the whirlpool between Italy and Sicily.

179   *Sidon:* a port in Lebanon.

193   *Furies:* the Eumenides, whose task it was to punish murder and other crimes, including perjury.

The Judgement of Zeus (203–7): God gives his assent to the prayer of Ariadne.

V. *Aegeus's Lament* (208–50): The father of Theseus unwittingly explains the mechanism by which the punishment prayed for by Ariadne and assented to by Zeus will be carried out.

228   *sacred Itonus:* a town in Thessaly, site of a famous sanctuary of the goddess Athena.

229   *Erectheus:* a mythical king of Athens.

241   *Acropolis:* the citadel of Athens.

VI. *Iacchus Searching for Ariadne* (251–65): the briefest of the four scenes on the coverlet. Ariadne in despair is sought by the god Dionysus, who will take her as his bride.

251   *Iacchus:* the name of a minor deity who came to be identified with Dionysus.

252   *Sileni* and *Satyrs:* the male attendants on Dionysus: Sileni (the plural of Silenus, originally the teacher and companion of the god) were pictured as bald, drunken old men with potbellies.

256   *Euhoe, Euhoe:* the ritual cry of the followers of Dionysus.

VII. *The Wedding Feast, Part II* (266–382) consists of three scenes: the departure of the mortal wedding guests (266–78), the arrival of the immortals (279–303), and the song of the Parcae (304–82).

280	*Chiron the Centaur:* In the traditional version of this story, Chiron gives the bride away and is also the tutor of the young Achilles.
281	*Favonian:* the Roman version of Zephyr, identified with the mild breezes of spring.
291–92	*the pliant sister of burnt-out Phaeton:* the poplar. Phaeton borrowed the chariot of his father, Helios, the Sun, but could not control the horses who drew it through the sky; blazing out of control, he was thunderbolted by Zeus. His sisters, the Heliades, wept so uncontrollably that they were turned into poplars, which, to this day weep the tears that Helios turns into amber.
295	*Prometheus:* After stealing fire from heaven, Prometheus was punished in the way that C. describes. One version of the story has him winning his freedom by warning Zeus of the prophecy about the son of Thetis.
300– 301	*Apollo:* The enmity of Apollo is not a usual part of the story. Fordyce says, "Catullus is following another version in which the death of Achilles at Apollo's hand . . . has coloured the earlier part of the story and Apollo's enmity is acknowledged from the beginning." Apollo's *sister* is Hecate, and Idrus is the name of the founder of Idrias, a town famous for its devotion to the goddess.
306	*the Parcae:* the Italian goddesses of fate, who spun, measured, and snipped the thread of life.
329	*Hesperus:* the evening star, at whose rising the marriage ceremony begins.
346	*Pelops:* obtained his bride Hippodamia by treachery and murder. His sons were Thyestes and Atreus, father of Agamemnon.
358	*Scamander:* the Trojan river. A reference to Achilles' activities in *The Iliad*, Book 23.
365	*the sacrificed virgin:* The ghost of Achilles orders the Greeks to sacrifice Polyxena, daughter of Priam and Hecuba, to be his bride in the underworld.
367	*Achaians:* the Greeks.
368	*Neptune:* The walls of Troy were said to have been built by Neptune.

VIII. *Conclusion* (383–410): C. draws a contrast between the Heroic Age, when gods and mortals mingled freely, even in the marriage bed, and the present age of moral degeneracy, when the gods are not seen at all.

391	*Liber:* Dionysus. *Parnassus:* a mountain north of Delphi.

396   *Triton:* a mythical lake, which different writers located in different places. *Nemesis, Virgin of Rhamnus:* the goddess charged with punishing transgressions such as murder and perjury. *Rhamnus:* the site of a famous shrine to the goddess in Attica.

65

The obligation to provide poems to friends who asked for them was one that C. took very seriously, as seen here and in poem 68. The movement of the poem, from grief to recovery, suggests that it was not written immediately after the brother's death.

2   *the poetic virgins:* the Muses.
4   *Ortalus:* possibly Quintus Hortensius Hortalus, an orator and poet.
6   *Lethe:* one of the rivers of the underworld. Those who set foot in it lost all memory of their previous lives.
8   *Troad; Rhoeteum:* Rhoeteum was a promontory in the Troad, the region along the Aegean coast in Asia Minor whose center was the city of Troy.
14   *Itylus:* the legendary son of Tereus and Procne. When Tereus ravaged Procne's sister Philomela, Procne slew Itylus. Pursued by Tereus, the sisters were saved when the gods turned Procne into a nightingale and her sister into a swallow.

66

The translation of Callimachus referred to in poem 65. Callimachus' poem originally belonged to a collection in which he accounted for the origins of things—in this case, how the constellation which we still call the *Coma Berenice* got its name. In 247 B.C., King Ptolemy III of Egypt married his cousin, Berenice, and shortly thereafter invaded Syria. Berenice vowed a lock of her hair for his safe return; but after being offered to the gods, the lock mysteriously vanished! What to do? Providentially, the astronomer Conon discovered that it had indeed been taken up to heaven and given a prominent place among the other stars. Callimachus expends a great deal of erudition on this pretty conceit, no doubt pleasing to Berenice, who lent her name to yet another important Alexandrian invention: varnish.

1   *he:* Conon.
5   *Love summons Trivia . . . :* When the moon is not visible in the sky, it is because she is visiting her mortal lover, Endymion, asleep in his cave on Mount Latmus.

22   *a brother:* Ptolemy and Berenice were actually cousins, but it was customary to speak of the King's consort as his sister.

43–46 *Thia* was the mother of Helios, the Sun. In 483 B.C., when the Persian king Xerxes was invading Greece, he dug a canal around, rather than through, Mount Athos.

48   *race of Chalybes:* a legendary tribe of miners and ironworkers who lived on the southeastern shore of the Black Sea. Kenneth Quinn notes that C. is describing the manufacturing of cast iron. (Quinn, p. 362)

52–57 *Memnon . . . Canopus:* the kind of passage that has made the term "Alexandrian" something less than an unqualified compliment. *Memnon* was the legendary son of Tithonus and Eos, and a king of Ethiopia. His brother *Zephyr*, the west wind, is imagined as a winged horse in the service of *Arsinoe*, Berenice's predecessor as queen of Egypt, who was deified after her death and identified with *Aphrodite;* her temple was located at *Zephyrium*, and so it is natural, pretends Callimachus, that Zephyr should do her bidding. Zephyr steals the lock of hair and conveys it to the temple of the goddess of love. Arsinoe was Greek, a Macedonian, and her temple was near *Canopus*, in Egypt.

61   *Ariadne:* Dionysus gave Ariadne a crown, which was placed in heaven when they were married.

63–67 The *Coma Berenice* is describing, accurately, her own position in reference to these other constellations.

70   *Tethys:* the wife of Oceanus. (See notes on 64, 30 and 31.)

71   *Rhamnusian Virgin:* the goddess Nemesis, who dealt out divine retribution to evildoers.

94   *Orion . . . Aquarius:* The presence of the *Coma* keeps these two constellations apart.

67

None of the characters mentioned in this poetic dialogue can be identified, though Caecilius might be the poet addressed in poem 35. The action takes place in Verona.

32–33 *Brixia . . . Mella:* Brixia (now Brescia) lies to the west of Sirmio, which is west of Verona. The Mella passes about a mile to the west of Brixia.

68

Poem 68 consists either of two poems meant for two different recipients or of one poem in two parts, both of which were meant for the same recipient; owing to insoluble textual problems, it isn't likely that we will ever know for certain what C. intended. I have opted to translate it as a single poem, addressed to someone named Allius, whose wife or mistress has either left him or died, and who consequently asks C. for some poems to console him in his troubles.

In the first forty lines, C. recapitulates Allius's troubles, expresses his regret for them, and explains that his own grief over the death of his brother, his dismay over Lesbia's infidelities, and his isolation in Verona all prevent him from complying. Just at the point where he appears to be hanging up on Allius, the poet suddenly launches into an invocation to the Muses: he is now determined to tell the world what Allius has done for him. The first forty lines were casual, chatty, unbuttoned: the remainder of the poem is elaborately structured, rich in its imagery, complex in its emotions, and thoroughly Alexandrian in its occasionally highstrung display of obscure erudition. The parallels between simplicity and complexity in the two parts of this poem and in poems 65 and 66 are intriguing.

10   *gifts of the Muses & Venus:* Much ingenuity has been spent by scholars trying to figure out what C. meant by this phrase. Perhaps Allius has asked for some poems, and, oh yes, some love poems as well.

15   *the toga of manhood:* C. would have put it on when he was fifteen or sixteen years old.

53–54   *Etna:* the volcano in Sicily. *Thermopylae:* the pass between northern and central Greece, named for its hot springs.

64   *Castor and Pollux:* the Dioscuri, heavenly twins charged with the protection of seafarers.

74   In the *Iliad, Protesilaus* is the first Greek to fall in the fighting at Troy. He had been married to *Laodamia* for only a single day when he went off to war. The neglected sacrifice that C. alludes to is not mentioned by Homer and is presumed to be a later accretion to the story.

109–16 *shafts . . . Cyllene:* After slaying the *man-eating birds of Stymphalia,* Hercules is said to have drilled underground channels near the town of Pheneus in Arcadia, in order to drain flood waters from the plain at the foot of Mount Cyllene. After his death, Hercules was granted immortality and the hand of the maiden goddess *Hebe* in marriage.

155   *Themis:* the goddess who represents divine justice in all relations to men.

69

Rufus is likely to have been Marcus Caelius Rufus.

74

Gellius may have been one L. Gellius Poplicola, about whom there circulated rumors of the kind that C. here elaborates upon. The specific nature of the offense that inspired this poem, as well as poems 80, 88, 90, 91, and 116, is unknown, but romantic rivalry does not seem an implausible cause.

77

Rufus is, once again, quite possibly M. Caelius Rufus.

78

Gallus is otherwise unknown.

79

Lesbius: if Lesbia is either the notorious Clodia or one of her two sisters, then Lesbius must be their brother, the infamous Publius Clodius Pulcher. C. puns on his cognomen, which means "pretty." A kiss on the lips was the customary greeting between men when they met on the street; C. is implying that Clodius's fondness for fellatio makes greeting him in this way a prospect to be shunned by most of his associates.

80

Victor is otherwise unknown.

81

Problems with Juventius. The houseguest from *Pisaurum*, a town in Umbria on the Adriatic coast, is unknown.

83

If Lesbia is Clodia Metelli, *her husband* would have been Quintus Metellus Celer, a distinguished patrician, who died in 59 B.C.

84

Arrius: "Arrius is a parvenu of humble origin who is uncertain of his aspirates and in his efforts to imitate educated speech inserts them in the wrong places. There is no reason to suppose the joke is more complicated." (Fordyce)

86

Quintia is otherwise unknown.

88

Tethys: wife of *Oceanus.* (See notes on poem 64, ll. 30 and 31.)

90

Incestuous marriage was believed to be customary among the Persian Magi.

93

Caesar is Gaius Julius Caesar.

94

Mentula is slang for "penis." This particular mentula is usually identified with Caesar's henchman, Mamurra. *The pot gathers its own potherbs:* apparently a proverbial expression.

95

An advertisement for the long-awaited poem of C.'s friend, Gaius Helvius *Cinna.* The work, which did not survive, was no doubt rather similar to C.'s poem 64, at least in size. Cinna's poem was a romance based on a suitably recondite, slightly twisted myth: the incestuous passion of Zmyrna for her father, Cinyras, and her metamorphosis into a tree whose trunk produces Adonis. *Hortensius* is possibly Quintus Hortentius Hortalus, principally known for his florid oratory. The *Annals of Volusius* are dumped on in poem 36. Antimachus was a poet condemned for his verbosity by Callimachus.

96

Quintilia was the mistress of Calvus.

97

Aemilius is otherwise unknown, and probably a good thing too.

98

Victius is unidentifiable.

Caelius may be M. Caelius Rufus. *Quintus* is perhaps the same Quintus who is addressed in poem 82. An *Aufilena* is cautioned in poems 110 and 111.

Cornelius may be the Nepos addressed in poem 1. *Silence:* the Egyptian god Harpocrates, depicted with a finger on his lips.

Silo is unidentifiable.

Tappo is unidentifiable.

The *mount of the chaste Muses:* Olympus.

Cominius is otherwise unknown.

Naso is otherwise unknown.

Maecilia is otherwise unknown, though some think that the name should be Mucilla, an affectionate diminutive for Mucia, Pompey's third wife. If so, then one of the charter lovers would have been Julius Caesar. *Pompey's first consulship:* 70 B.C. He was consul again in 55 B.C.

114

Firmum: a town (now Fermo) on the Adriatic coast.

115

Croesus: a Lydian king whose wealth became proverbial.

THE POEMS OF CATULLUS

Designed by Ann Walston

Composed by G&S Typesetters, Inc.
in Palatino text and display

Printed by The Maple Press Company
on 50-lb. Glatfelter Eggshell Cream